and beginning with MOSES ...

John R Cross

and beginning with MOSES …

Teaching those who know
little or nothing about the Bible.

Edition 2

Copyright © 2007 by GoodSeed® International

Published by GoodSeed® International
P.O. Box 3704, Olds, AB, T4H 1P5 Canada
Email: info@goodseed.com

ISBN 978-1-890082-64-2

🍁 Printed in Canada

*"And beginning with Moses and all the Prophets,
he explained to them
what was said in all the Scriptures
concerning himself."*
Luke 24:27

index

the preface

It was Sunday, 2000 years ago, the day of the resurrection of Jesus Christ. As two of his disciples traveled the road from Jerusalem to Emmaus, they were joined by Jesus Himself, but they did not recognize Him. He asked them,

"What are you discussing together as you walk along?"

They stood still, their faces downcast. One of them, named Cleopas, asked him, "Are you only a visitor to Jerusalem and do not know the things that have happened there in these days?"

"What things?" he asked.

"About Jesus of Nazareth," they replied. "He was a prophet, powerful in word and deed before God and all the people. The chief priests and our rulers handed him over to be sentenced to death, and they crucified him; but we had hoped that he was the one who was going to redeem Israel. And what is more, it is the third day since all this took place. In addition, some of our women amazed us. They went to the tomb early this morning but didn't find his body. They came and told us that they had seen a vision of angels, who said he was alive. Then some of our companions went to the tomb and found it just as the women had said, but him they did not see."

He said to them, "How foolish you are, and how slow of heart to believe all that the prophets have spoken! Did not the Christ have to suffer these things and then enter his glory?" And beginning with Moses and all the Prophets, he explained to them what was said in all the Scriptures concerning himself.

Luke 24:14-27

What a lesson that must have been! I hope to hear it myself someday, from the Savior!

The ministry of GOODSEED International was started for the purpose of creating tools that communicate the Bible's message using the same approach Jesus used on the road to Emmaus. We begin at the beginning. We begin with Moses and all the prophets. The following pages answer the why, what, where, when and how of that approach. As we create more tools and gain more experience, we will not only enlarge this book but add to the series of which this is the first volume.

In writing anything about methods of evangelism, we need to preface our thoughts with what the Scripture says:

> *"Not by might nor by power, but by my Spirit," says the LORD Almighty.*   *Zechariah 4:6*

I believe it is enjoined upon the believer to communicate the Word of God clearly, for faith comes only through understanding the Word, yet the process of communication is not independent of the Spirit's working. Some of the ideas you will read in this booklet are just that, ideas. Look upon them as being helpful suggestions. Others are well founded in the Word. Those we best not ignore. For both, we need to ask God to bless our efforts with the mighty working of His Spirit.

John R. Cross

a real problem

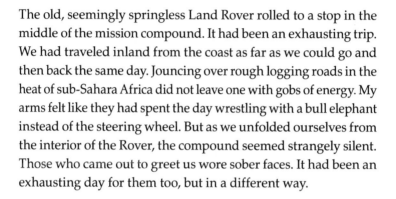

The old, seemingly springless Land Rover rolled to a stop in the middle of the mission compound. It had been an exhausting trip. We had traveled inland from the coast as far as we could go and then back the same day. Jouncing over rough logging roads in the heat of sub-Sahara Africa did not leave one with gobs of energy. My arms felt like they had spent the day wrestling with a bull elephant instead of the steering wheel. But as we unfolded ourselves from the interior of the Rover, the compound seemed strangely silent. Those who came out to greet us wore sober faces. It had been an exhausting day for them too, but in a different way.

Early that morning as the dust settled after our departure, the tribal village had begun to seethe with emotion. A small delegation showed up at the missionaries' house and warned them to stay indoors. It seemed that the chief had been sick; nothing life threatening, but a little *under the weather* nonetheless. An old lady—known as a prophetess—had discerned the source of the chief's fever. God had apparently told her that three different young men had worked sorcery on him. The guilty three were brought before the village leaders to see what they had to say about it. Vehemently, the accused denied such an allegation. Many in the village did not believe them. Others defended them. Feelings were running high. The delegation made it clear to the missionaries that they were to stay out of sight. This they did, but they also peered through the cracks in their tribal house to see what would happen next.

What they witnessed next was ancient by origin, going back deep into tribal roots—it was a *trial by ordeal*. The accused were stripped and made to drink a foamy poison, pounded from the bark of a sasswood tree. Then the fluid was poured—forced would be a better term—into every orifice of the body. It was a disgusting, crude, vulgar process. One victim immediately threw up the repulsive liquid. He lived. But as the missionaries peered between the cracks in their home, they watched the other two men stagger around the village until they collapsed. They were dead by noon.

As the sun set, this was the somber report that greeted us as we crawled out of the confines of the Land Rover. I remember being somewhat dumbfounded. Was not this a village that claimed to be "Christian?" Missionaries[1] had "evangelized" these people decades ago. Indeed the whole country was speckled with church steeples. Even the local taxis and stores had Bible verses plastered on them. Many a mission leader would have flaunted this country as a mission's success story. But here was a trial by ordeal—a poisoning of three healthy men with sasswood.

Although I knew that this particular form of *trial by ordeal* had a long history in West Africa,[2] one would think that when the people overwhelmingly accepted Christianity, such rituals would have been relegated to the dusty past. Not so.

The next day, I, along with several others, informally interviewed members of the village. I remember the church pastor explaining to us in detail how the poison was made and administered. He was very matter-of-fact—it obviously being the accepted way to deal with such problems. When the pastor explained how the two men died, I asked him if they had indeed been guilty of sorcery. He was strong in his affirmation. He assured us that they were guilty, not only because they had died, but also because they had been fingered by God himself through the church prophetess. He even doubted the innocence of the man who survived.

As I listened to the story, I could see the telltale traits of a problem that has plagued missions for centuries. It is a phenomenon called *syncretism.*

Decades ago, the villagers were taught the Bible by a missionary who did not know their heart language—he spoke the trade language only. Typically speaking, tribal people do not understand trade languages very well, so the message they heard was not clear to them. Nonetheless the villagers enthusiastically embraced "Christianity." They simply added what they thought the Bible said to what they already believed. They combined the two and ended up with a third religion, a syncretization of two very different world views.

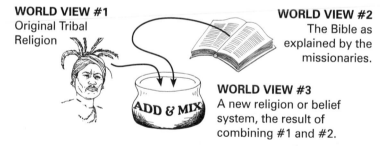

WORLD VIEW #1
Original Tribal
Religion

WORLD VIEW #2
The Bible as
explained by the
missionaries.

ADD & MIX

WORLD VIEW #3
A new religion or belief
system, the result of
combining #1 and #2.

This new religion had an abundance of outward Christian trappings— pastors, prophetesses, prayer, church meetings and steeples, with Bible verses plastered on everything from truck bumpers to store fronts—but inwardly the people retained much of their original tribal beliefs. *Trial by ordeal* was dramatic evidence of something amiss, but there was much, much more. For example, further questioning revealed that the Bible verses were simply fetishes to ward off evil spirits. The prophetess was a reworked edition of the tribal sorcerer. On and on it went. The evidence for a mixing of belief systems was everywhere. Syncretism was rampant.

Isolated case? Unfortunately not.

SYNCRETISM

Syncretism is a huge problem in missions. This is not an exaggeration. For example, in some places in the world, it is reported that vast numbers of people have converted to Christianity. Certain evangelistic organizations, pumping out glossy magazines, show bar graphs protruding from world maps, indicating the numbers coming to the Lord each day. I remember reading one such magazine in the mid-70's. Curiosity got the best of me and, doing some calculations, I figured out that if the conversions were to continue at the stated rate, the entire world would be saved well before the millennium. As we well know, this has not happened. Are these conversions no more than paper statistics? Well, I would be loathe to accuse anyone of falsifying records, but I think we can safely say that time has proven that a significant number of these "converts" are highly syncretized "believers." Some consider these folk "Christians" whereas others say that there is *no way* they can be "saved."

One would think that with the immensity of the problem, this would be the primary prayer request, the most talked about issue at mission conferences. But the truth is, few Christians even know what the word syncretism means. Though the situation is improving, I have found that even at the college and seminary level, many people cannot explain the concept of syncretism. As to how it relates to missions, it holds an even greater mystery.

There is a good reason why syncretism remains in the shadows. It is a touchy issue, especially at mission conferences. I remember a missionary explaining it to me.

- **Mission Board A:** The representative from this board will tell you that he hasn't learned the people's heart language.[3] He will tell you, *"Sure, using the trade language has its drawbacks, but as far as communicating the gospel, it works just fine."* He has mastered various forms of mass evangelism. When, at the missions' conference, he gets up to give his report, he talks about thousands coming to the Lord—an immense turning to God. The audience is electrified by his reports. It is exactly what all Christians want to hear.

- **Mission Board B:**[4] The representative from "B" just happens to minister in the same country as "A." This missionary has spent years learning the heart language of the people. He knows the culture—what the people think. He knows that most of the "thousands turning to Christ" are not true *born from above* believers. Rather they are people who have added a veneer of Christianity to their old beliefs. It looks good on the outside, but behind it all is plain old paganism.

This missionary has led many to the Lord as well, but he cannot point to thousands. What is he to do? If he tells the truth about what is going on, he will expose "A" and then it may appear he has "sour grapes" because he hasn't had the same success. He also knows that the folk in Mission Board "A" mean well—they are doing what they think is right—and there is no doubt that there have been some genuine conversions. He feels in a lose-lose predicament. So he does what most missionaries do. He skirts the problem in his report and says nothing of syncretism.

In the meantime the local church continues on in its blessed ignorance—ignorant of what happens when sasswood, fetishes and sorcerers are mixed with the Bible.

SYNCRETISM IN THE BIBLE

Syncretism is not new. The ancient Israelites en route from Egypt to the Promised Land had problems in this area. God asked them a rhetorical question.

> *"Did you present Me with sacrifices and grain offerings in the wilderness for forty years, O house of Israel?" Amos 5:25 NASB*

The answer was, "Yes, they did." They could make a legitimate claim to be following the true God. But there was something more. The next verse explains what they carried in their bags. God said…

> *"You also carried along Sikkuth your king and Kiyyun, your images, the star of your gods which you made for yourselves."*
> *Amos 5:26 NASB*

These were pagan Assyrian gods. Israel was trying to worship God and idols at the same time. They were mixing two belief systems.

This problem of "mixing" seems innate to the human heart. When centuries ago, Gentiles settled in the heartland of Israel, the Bible says,

> *They worshiped the LORD, **but they also** appointed all sorts of their own people to officiate for them as priests in the shrines at the high places.* 2 Kings 17:32

Visiting the Middle East, I remember pondering those ancient high place altars, recalling God's grief with the immorality and child sacrifice that was often part of idolatrous worhip. The Lord said,

> *"They have built the high places of Baal to burn their sons in the fire as offerings to Baal—something I did not command or mention, nor did it enter my mind."*   Jeremiah 19:5

Rightly so, such decadence had *not* entered God's mind, but man's mind seemed quite agile at mixing this evil and God's good. The Bible says,

> *They worshiped the LORD, **but they also** served their own gods in accordance with the customs of the nations from which they had been brought.*   2 Kings 17:33

This is syncretism. Syncretism's tenacity is illustrated in that, even after the Gentile "settlers" were instructed in true worship,

> *They would not listen, however, but persisted in their former practices. **Even while these people were worshiping the LORD, they were serving their idols.***   2 Kings 17:40,41

Centuries later God had the Apostle Paul write…

> *"… I do not want you to become sharers in demons. You cannot drink the cup of the Lord **and** the cup of demons; you cannot partake of the table of the Lord **and** the table of demons."*
>   1 Corinthians 10:20-21

Syncretism has plagued the church since its earliest days. Paul wrote the book of Galatians to sort out the confusion caused by those who were trying to mix religious legalism with the truth. The book of Colossians and the First Epistle of John were written for a similar purpose, this time having to do with a mixing of Gnosticism and the Bible. In the following centuries, people syncretized true Christianity with ancient Roman, Egyptian and Babylonian paganism, creating various "mixes" dominated by error. Mohammed syncretized Arab tribal beliefs with Judaism and a Christian cult to form Islam. These religions in turn have syncretized to form others. The list is long. It seems very *human* to believe a mangled and mixed message.

LANGUAGE AND CULTURE

Syncretism is caused by many things, not the least being that man has a propensity to reject or suppress God's truth. (Roman 1:18) However, much syncretism can be blamed on poor communication.

To communicate clearly, it helps to have a shared heart language and culture. Though this can hardly be mandatory in all situations, an understanding of the problems that develop when using second or trade languages is critical.[5] There are legitimate situations for teaching the Bible in a trade language, but it must be done carefully with a mechanism in place to double-check comprehension. Obviously, it is important to remove as much of the language and cultural barrier as possible. But even when one shares the same language, misunderstandings can occur leading to syncretism.

SHORTCUTS

For example, in our "western" societies we usually share a common language and culture. Having that common ground gives one a great leap forward in removing the confusion that leads to syncretism. But we still have a problem. Our western culture is cursed with a tyrant in the shape of a clock. It is hard to get people to sit down and listen to a reasoned explanation of the Bible. Life is rushed. Thus we Christians have resorted to short sermons and even briefer gospel tracts to communicate the gospel message.

But when you stop and think about it, most of us agree that a rushed message is often a misunderstood message—either because the necessary facts are too sparse, or because in our rush we cannot communicate the gravity of the message. Whether we recognize it or not, our western society is a set-up for syncretism, and since syncretism is hardest to spot in one's own culture, many deny it even exists. That just compounds the problem.

No one will deny that brief messages and gospel tracts have worked to a certain extent, but probably that has been because our society in the past had a basic knowledge of the Bible. Not too many years ago, most people on the street had a reasonably good idea of who God was, what sin was, and that God judged sin. In those days, a gospel tract gathered together details already in the reader's mind, fleshing out a skeleton of thought that already existed. But much has changed. Nowadays, the skeleton is often non-existent. As our society has moved into the post-Christian era, we have been confronted with people who are totally illiterate of the Scriptures. Often, without us realizing it, our shortcuts have created more confusion than understanding.

If we were to know the truth, many of our methods of evangelism have contributed to syncretism right here in our own backyard. Those with a knowledge of syncretism who are willing to step back and take a hard look at western "Christianity," realize we have a problem. It is not easy to accept that reality. We often sincerely deny it, for it's hard to see it in ourselves. We don't like being told that we have a "confusion" problem anymore than Mission Board "A" likes hearing about it, but in many cases that is the truth. But before we are too hard on ourselves, let me conclude with a story.

In Lystra there sat a man crippled in his feet, who was lame from birth and had never walked. He listened to Paul as he was speaking **[in Greek, the trade language of the area]**. *Paul looked directly at him, saw that he had faith to be healed and called out, "Stand up on your feet!" At that, the man jumped up and began to walk.*

When the crowd saw what Paul had done, they shouted in the Lycaonian language, **[their heart language, a language Paul did not know]** *"The gods have come down to us in human form!" Barnabas they called Zeus, and Paul they called Hermes because he was the chief speaker. The priest of Zeus, whose temple was just outside the city, brought bulls and wreaths to the city gates because he and the crowd wanted to offer sacrifices to them.* **[The Lycaonians responded positively, but they mixed their religion with Paul's message!]**

But when the apostles Barnabas and Paul heard of this **[as it was translated for them]**, *they tore their clothes and rushed out into the crowd* **[of Lycaonians]**, *shouting* **[in Greek]**: *"Men, why are you doing this? We too are only men, human like you. We are bringing you good news, telling you to turn from these worthless things to the living God, who made heaven and earth and sea and everything in them. In the past, he let all nations go their own way. Yet he has not left himself without testimony: He has shown kindness by giving you rain from heaven and crops in their seasons; he provides you with plenty of food and fills your hearts with joy." Even with these words* **[in Greek]**, *they had difficulty keeping the crowd from sacrificing to them* **[because the Lycaonians could not understand Greek very well]**. *Acts 14:8-18*

Those of us who have spent years overseas can chuckle a little, thinking of the times we have experienced similar confusion.

You can see Paul, frantic to correct the situation, shouting, as if speaking louder would make the message clear. And then there are the Lycaonians, smiling and nodding at the babbling missionaries, and continuing right on with the sacrifice. Oh my! If misery loves company, we can draw relief from this story.

But then we need to be mature enough to look for a solution.

[1] The missionaries who witnessed the events had moved into the village, assuming that either the people were very confused on the gospel or had never understood it in the first place. They were recent newcomers, not connected with those who had originally "evangelized" this area.

[2] In the book, "Barrow's Boys" (Atlantic Monthly Press ©1998 Fergus Fleming), Fergus Fleming tells of the British manservant turned explorer, Richard Lemon Lander, who reported a court of ordeal he witnessed in West Africa (c.1831). The *"King gave final judgement by means of a poisoned drink. If the offender lived he was innocent, if he died he was guilty. Very few lived, as Lander learned when he peeked inside the hut and saw that it was lined with skulls."* Lander himself was tried by ordeal. He reported the drink as 'bitter and disagreeable.' When he did not die instantly, he dizzily made his way back to his hut to discreetly take an emetic. His stomach obliged and got rid of the sasswood poison. He lived.

[3] The *heart language* is usually the language spoken in the home, in which abstract concepts such as love and sin are understood. In contrast, the *trade language* deals with the concrete, such as pots and pans. It is usually reserved for the marketplace.

[4] It is highly simplistic to divide "missions" into two camps. Many organizations legitimately apply both methods in their outreach. There are also a whole spectrum of methods and ministries which are not mentioned, that might best fit between the two given above. Rather than discuss the many methods with their varying degrees of effectiveness, I picked two common approaches in an effort to define the issue clearly for those unacquainted with the larger issues at stake.

[5] Those involved in ESL (English as a Second Language) ministries need to be well informed about the problems of syncretism.

CHAPTER 2

a biblical solution

Yes, we have a problem—but anyone can point out problems. Is there a biblical solution? Is there anything we can do to avoid syncretism in our presentation of the gospel message? I believe there is a solution.

WHAT IS THE GOSPEL?

To begin with, as Christians we need to realize that syncretism is compounded by our own biblical ignorance of what the Scripture teaches on the gospel. I find an appallingly low level of comprehension when it comes to doctrines such as substitution, justification, redemption, and propitiation. Many believers have no solid theological foundations. Anyone who has been around long enough to follow trends, knows that this problem is increasing.

So what's to be done about it? Simply put, as believers we need to commit ourselves to a continuing study of God's Word, a study that moves beyond the superficial. Believers need to get into the Word and grapple with the meat.

As worldly post-modern values have been syncretized with biblical values, it has become the "in thing" to not take a strong stand on anything more than the bare essentials. Even the essentials have suffered. The world may prefer to live in the gray zone, but generally speaking, the Bible is black and white. We can and should speak about absolutes, even in biblical details. There are areas of Scripture where honest differences of opinion exist, but even in those areas we need to have some form of conviction.

Unfortunately, people have adopted a post-modern view of Scripture where it has become wrong to say something is right or wrong. What we really need are convictions, even in the details, and where we have differences with other believers, we must disagree without being disagreeable. To have thrown overboard solid convictions for some sort of shaky unity is sheer folly.

Unity will only truly exist when we have a common doctrine and focus. To seek unity any other way is to open oneself to the subtle pressures of compromise. We may feel more comfortable mixing worldly post-modern values with the Bible, but it is not right. God hates it. We end up having Assyrian idols in our spiritual luggage.

Biblical illiteracy in the church has led to an understanding of the gospel that is as shallow as a raindrop, often emphasizing extra-biblical concepts and rituals in place of truth. This is tragic. At minimum, every believer should be able to explain simply and clearly what the Bible says about substitution and justification. If taught properly, even little children can understand and explain these doctrines clearly.

So to begin with, we need to get back into the Word and make sure we ourselves are grounded in what the gospel is, and what it isn't. We need to study out the meaning of words such as *justification, propitiation* and *redemption*—we need to grapple with the reality of the *substitutionary work of Christ*. Being clear on the gospel ourselves is the first step towards communicating it clearly to others.

DON'T ASSUME TOO MUCH

Secondly, to avoid syncretism we need to face the fact that our western, Christian-based society has changed. No longer does the average Joe on the street have a basic knowledge of the character of God, the nature of sin, and the historical reality of Jesus Christ.

I was teaching a couple in an evangelistic Bible study awhile back. Both were highly educated individuals. As the study progressed through creation, I brought out the fact that for someone to make this world, that individual had to be very intelligent, immensely powerful and everywhere present. As I continued with the lesson, all of a sudden the husband interrupted, "*Stop, stop, stop. You are talking about God as if he were a being—like a person.*" I acknowledged that to be true.

He then told me, "*I have never thought of God as being a person. I always thought of him as some sort of force.*"

Now think about the implications. Gravity is a force. If you are witnessing to a person who thinks **God** is some sort of force field like **gravity**, every time you say the word "God" you have confusion. For example, try sharing John 3:16. You start by saying, "*For **God** so loved the world ...*" You know exactly what you mean, but your listeners, listening through the grid of their world view, hear something like this, "*For **gravity** so loved the world ...*" Confusion!!

As North Americans, we need to wake up to the real world in which we live, a world missionaries have struggled against for years; a world where God is understood in a pantheistic sort of way—as a nebulous unifying force; where sin is relative—it's what you think it to be; and where they think the words "Jesus Christ" are a figure of speech—like "good grief."

In talking to people about their witnessing approach, I find many who assume too much in the listener's frame of reference. This should concern us. The listener may accept what we say, but will combine our statements about God with his or her understanding of who God is, and the result will be confusion—syncretism. If, unaware to you, your student has mixed *gravity* and *God*, there is no way that he or she will have a right understanding of the gospel message.

If, unaware to you, your student has mixed **gravity** and **God**, there is no way that he or she will have a **right understanding** of the gospel message.

A few years ago, a co-worker and I had an opportunity to share the gospel with a lady in her late 20's. She had gone through a very tough time in her teen years and was seeking answers for life. For two-and-a-half hours we applied our best evangelistic efforts to the situation. We carefully explained the gospel message several times. After she left, we both felt that we had been quite clear on the message and stopped to thank the Lord for the opportunity.

This lady did not become a believer at that time, but she did agree to a Bible study. During the study it was evident she knew virtually nothing about the Bible. After she became a believer, I asked her what had been her understanding of the message at the end of the initial two-and-a-half hours. I was appalled as she explained what she had understood by our careful explanation of the gospel. Her concept of our message was more akin to a bizarre cult than the Word of God. She had thoroughly syncretized what we had taught her. Her problem was that she just didn't have enough biblical information in her mind to make sense of what we were carefully telling her.

In North America, this sort of illiteracy is more common than the reverse. For several years, I had students interview ten people, choosing as much as possible those unlike themselves in background, age, culture, education, and so forth. They had to ask nine questions covering three areas of world view. The interviewer could not express his or her opinion on any of the answers. I asked them to remain as objective as possible. Here are the questions.

1) God:
   - When you hear the word "God," what comes to mind?
   - What would you say God is like?
   - Where did you get your ideas about God?

2) Man:
   - Why does man die?
   - What happens to man when he dies?
   - Where did you get your ideas about man and his future?

3) Right and Wrong (sin):
   - In life, what is right, and what is wrong (sin)? Name a few examples of each.
   - Are there any consequences for doing wrong (sin)? If so, what would those consequences be?
   - If someone says you are wrong about what is right and wrong—who decides who is right?

The results of these interviews revealed a level of biblical ignorance and syncretistic confusion that rivaled any foreign mission field on earth.

So what's to be done? Does that mean we should stop going to foreign countries and instead concentrate on preaching the gospel at home? Not at all, but it does mean we may do well to bring home from the mission field the lessons we have learned in reaching the biblically-illiterate. More on this later.

So, not only do we need to be clear on the gospel message ourselves, but we also must be conscious that we don't assume too much in our listeners understanding of the Bible. But let's move on.

What else should we be aware of to avoid syncretism?

BRIEF IS NOT BEST

Thirdly, to avoid syncretism we need to move beyond the McDonald's mindset in evangelism. Our culture may want everything fast—large fries and a strawberry shake to go, PLEASE!—but anything worthwhile, anything with value, will find people slowing down and taking more time. For example, when a couple buys a house, they usually do quite a bit of research and shopping around before they commit themselves. Most big decisions are not spur of the moment decisions—and they usually aren't made on a minimum of knowledge. For major decisions, going slow and being informed is the rule of thumb that people follow.

In contrast to this, we show up and present the gospel—involving the biggest decision one can make in an entire lifetime—and we present the whole shebang in fifteen minutes. For many, not only do we create a situation ripe for syncretism, but we reduce the seriousness of the message. We make it cheap.

Now don't get me wrong. I'm not saying that we should never give a brief gospel presentation. In some situations it may be the only choice we have. And I am not saying it never works—many of us know those who became believers through reading a gospel tract. But what I am saying is this: in a biblically-illiterate society, I don't believe brevity can be our standard procedure without significant confusion—without potential cost.

Is there a cost? Well, yes, possibly. Think of those people who thought they understood our message, but didn't, resulting in an inoculation towards further investigation of the truth. Think of those who tried to understand what we were saying but because of the rush were confused and left thinking that none of it made sense anyway. When the cost is considered…well, at minimum, it should cause one to pause and ponder, *"Am I sowing with care? Or, am I just blundering around?"*

DON'T REINVENT THE WHEEL

Finally, it would seem wise to learn from those who have grappled with syncretism problems overseas—those missionaries and mission boards who would identify themselves with mission board "B." They have been working for years with people who know nothing about the Bible. They have lived in a world that has never known Christianity. It can be rightly said that these missionaries have a gut-level feel for the dynamics of communicating in a post-Christian society.

Even more important than "picking the brains" of missionaries, is the determination to do a thorough study of Scripture to see what it has to say about the mixing of truth and error, and what solutions it offers—solutions that may have been overlooked. In a sense, *pick the minds* of the prophets. A good place to start is in Acts 17 where Paul addresses the Athenians—a people who knew not God.

In embarking on this study, one must remember that "syncretism" is a touchy subject. Even confronting the problem in the most gentle manner may offend some. But it must be done, or the church will drift into an ever-increasing whirlpool of double-think, syncretizing biblical truth with mysticism, psychology, paleontology, big business techniques, and the like. The pond is already muddy; it will soon become as black as coal. If you don't believe it, ask yourself where the vibrant church of Turkey, North Africa and much of Europe has gone. When you visit these countries, the 'black as coal' idiom seems an understatement.

Of course, many Christians have been trying various methods to get the message across to our post-Christian world. In the early 1980's attention began to focus on a seemingly new way to teach the Bible. New Tribes Mission was finding it an effective means to teach tribal people a clear gospel—a spectrum of the world that has had its shares of struggles with syncretism. Since tribal people know nothing of the Bible, this approach by necessity addressed those issues that exist in a biblically-illiterate society. This format of Bible teaching was found to be extremely effective in countering the confusion that results in syncretism and reaching those ignorant of the Bible.

As the western world became more and more secular with the onset of the post-Christian era, there were those familiar with this approach that felt it could be adapted and put into use in developed countries. In 1996, GoodSeed International began as an organization to coordinate, disseminate and create tools using this approach to teaching.

Among other things, this format of Bible study has been called:

- The Chronological Approach
- The Redemptive-Historical Approach
- The Narrative Approach
- Firm Foundations
- The Scarlet Thread of Redemption
- Storytelling the Bible
- God's Story
- World View Evangelism

Although GOODSEED uses all of the above labels, organizationally it has chosen to call it TERM—THE EMMAUS ROAD MESSAGE. Whatever the name, essentially they all share similar characteristics though the stories used to accomplish their purpose may differ slightly.

Though GOODSEED is one of the primary movers behind this form of teaching, one needs to understand that those involved in the organization do not feel that this is the only way Christians should do evangelism. However, they do believe it is a good way having many solid scriptural precedents. They also feel that it is something others should learn to use, especially when dealing with those who are biblically-illiterate. No mechanic keeps just screwdrivers in his toolbox. He has an assortment of tools to fit different situations. In the same way, we need to be acquainted with different approaches to communicating the gospel. This is especially true when a method has a strong biblical basis.

So what does GOODSEED specifically mean when talking about a TERM Bible study? In essentials, TERM is a MESSAGE told using a particular METHOD, having specific GOALS in mind.

THE MESSAGE:

Any message has its *irreducible minimums*—the core of the message. If you fail to communicate those key essentials then you have not passed on the message accurately. Below are four irreducible minimums that must be communicated if the gospel is to be understood.

- **A Holy God:** God exists in all His majesty, being the Creator-Owner of the Universe. He is a loving, caring God but *equally* He is also a holy lawgiver. His holiness demands that His law be kept perfectly. He can have nothing to do with any lawbreaker. *Only perfect people can live with a perfect God.*

- **A Helpless Sinner:** I was born into the world a lawbreaker, alienated from God. *I am far from perfect.* God's law says that all sin demands the death penalty. Not only do I die physically but I face something the Bible calls the *second death*—an eternity of suffering in the Lake of Fire. Since I am a sinner, there is no way I can avoid death. I am helpless.

- **A Sufficient Substitute:** Jesus, God Himself, came to this earth to live as a man. *He was perfect—sinless.* Because He had no sin of his own to die for, He could die for someone else's sin. In His love, He died in my place—taking the consequences of my sin on Himself. As evidenced by Jesus' resurrection, God accepted that death as an overwhelmingly sufficient payment for my sin—a fulfillment of the requirement of His holy law.

- **A Personal Faith:** I believe that when Jesus died on the cross, He died in my place. I rest in the fact that He alone has saved me from the judgment on my sin. *In Him, my resurrected Savior, I now have a perfection that is not my own, but is counted as mine because I trust Him.*[1] I will enjoy life with God both now and forever in Heaven.

These four essentials are the irreducible minimums of the gospel message. You want to communicate nothing less. Your students can forget other information, but when teaching the gospel, you definitely want them to remember these four facts.

THE METHOD:

In communicating a message, the methods are seemingly endless. By method we are not referring to the *means*, which could range from the spoken word to smoke signals and drums. Rather we are talking about *how* the message is arranged in the process of passing it on. For example, is the message communicated topically, word by word, as a narrative, systematically, or by "leaping around?" All of these are dynamics that define a method—or lack of a method. Below are four principles of communication that we believe describe a good way to pass on the gospel message. In stating these principles, we do not believe this is the only way that the Gospel can be taught, but we do feel it is a scriptural way.

- **The Story-Telling Principle:** One does not read a story by starting halfway through the book, jumping to the last chapter and then wrapping it up on page one. But much Bible study is built on that approach. TERM starts at the beginning of the story and then works its way through the Bible to a satisfactory completion. In other words, you get the whole story—the whole picture.[2]

   Studying the Bible sequentially gives an order to key information. For example, starting at the beginning with Creation, we learn who God is and much of what he is like. The Bible tells us that...

   "The heavens declare the glory of God..."   Psalm 19:1

Knowing what God is like is critical information, foundational to understanding all other biblical truths. It's useless to recite John 3:16 to someone who believes the sun is god or that God is an impersonal force such as gravity.

Apart from and accurate **understanding** of who God is, the **person** and the **work** of Jesus Christ is totally irrelevant to the man on the street

---

Continuing in Genesis, Chapter 3 explains to us how sin entered the world. Here we get the first glimpse of man's predicament and God's solution. Without this vital information the Bible does not make any sense at all.

As we progress chronologically through the Scripture, other doctrines are placed in perspective. For example, the Bible presents the Ten Commandments given at Mount Sinai before it presents God's grace shown on Mount Calvary. This is significant. It is through the law that man becomes aware of his sinful condition.

… through the law we become conscious of sin. Romans 3:20

Of course man's sinful condition is only significant if he already knows quite a bit about God's character, that He is holy and cannot allow sin in His presence. Understanding the law creates an awareness of one's lostness. It is at that point that the law becomes …

… our schoolmaster to bring us unto Christ, that we might be justified by faith.   Galatians 3:24

When man understands that he is lost then he is much more likely to seek a way to be saved.[3]

> To get **saved** a person
> must first know that he is **lost**.

When talking about teaching the Bible *chronologically*, it is important to understand that TERM is not solely a telling of biblical stories sequentially. There are many books that give a chronological presentation of the Bible, and yet they do not communicate what we are thinking of when we talk about THE EMMAUS ROAD MESSAGE. Those sequential Bible stories must be tied together using the other three principles below.

• **The Mathematical Principle:** Another key to understanding the Bible is to build from the foundation up—a very simple educational concept! You don't start children in kindergarten by teaching them algebra. Rather, you begin with basic numbers and move from the simple to the complex. If you skip the fundamentals, even rudimentary algebra will be beyond your grasp. It's the same way with the Bible. If you neglect the foundations, your understanding of the Bible will be confused. Though teaching chronologically tends to put the foundational material in the right order—simple to complex—one still needs to keep this principle of learning in mind. But TERM teaching is more that just having good foundations.

> You don't start children in **kindergarten**
> by teaching them **algebra**.

- **The Priority Principle:** The Bible is a thick book with incredible detail, but not all its information is equally important. The message found in John 3:16 is of greater significance than that contained in the entire book of the Song of Solomon. Both are scripture, both are profitable for the soul, but the message found in John 3:16 should have priority when teaching a novice about the Bible.

Though far from comprehensive, TERM covers key biblical events—**important ones**, enhancing understanding by stringing them together in logical sequence—like hanging clothes spaced apart on a clothesline. Though this clothesline of comprehension does not cover every story, the events you do study are significant, and when tied together, can be seen as explaining one very, very important message.

It is absolutely critical that one not muddy that message by getting off on sidetracks, "bogging down" in details, or dragging out the study over long periods of time. Why?

a) The gospel is an emergency message sent from Heaven telling a person how he may be rescued. Lifesaving messages are usually communicated with urgency. If you "putter around," the message will lose its importance in the mind of the listener. Inadvertently, you will be making a major message into a minor story.

b) If you take too long or get "bogged down," your Bible study will lose its sense of progression and continuity. The key points will not tie together in your student's mind. You will end up teaching a number of individual Bible lessons instead of one message that ties together.

You must make consistent progress on the major points, or the study will lose its perspective and momentum. The urgency and thus the importance of the message will be lost.

Understanding this dynamic cannot be overstated. To know how to major on the majors—to get the most important information across—is critical to the success of the study.

> To know how to **major** on the **majors** is
> critical to the sucess of the study.

- **The Clarity Principle:** There are only a few key themes that run through the entire Bible (Salvation, Sanctification, and Glorification). If you mix them together you get confusion. (i.e. Sanctificational truth mixed with Salvation can end up with a "works salvation.") TERM focuses on only one theme. In so doing, it brings together many diverse topics in the Bible, but because there is only one theme, those topics are covered in such a way that they fit together. In addressing that one single theme, we apply the other three points of TERM resulting in remarkable clarity as it pertains to the person and work of Christ.

THE MESSAGE USING THE METHOD

When we combine the MESSAGE with the METHOD, we call that approach to communication THE EMMAUS ROAD MESSAGE (TERM).

The
Emmaus
Road
Message

TERM teaching clearly cuts through the problems caused by syncretism—sorting out truth from error—by handing the learner a tidbit of information at a time. That tidbit is so small that it cannot be misunderstood. When all the tidbits are put together in sequential order, they present an overwhelmingly logical explanation of the truth. A clear gospel is a powerful gospel. But notice that it is only powerful if the message is understood clearly. Paul, in the book written to the Romans, wrote:

> I am not ashamed of the gospel, because it is the **power** of God for the salvation of everyone who believes … Romans 1:16

The word *power* is the Greek word *dunamis* which means *power, might, strength*. It is the word from which we get the English word *dynamite*. But notice how the word *dunamis* is translated elsewhere.

> If then I do not grasp the **meaning [dunamis]** of what someone is saying, I am a foreigner to the speaker, and he is a foreigner to me.　　　　　　　1 Corinthians 14:11

If we are to understand the Scriptures correctly, it would seem that the *power* of the gospel is directly connected to having understood the *meaning* of the gospel. So, we not only want to be clear on the MESSAGE ourselves, but we also want to use a METHOD that ensures we have accurately communicated that message—a method that makes sure the listener has understood exactly what we are saying. That is our goal.

The **power** of the gospel is directly connected to having **understood** the **meaning** of the gospel.

THE GOAL

In teaching TERM, we have five goals in mind.[4]

Accuracy: It is the goal of TERM to present a clear gospel presentation. Experience has taught us that a very great number of "believers" in North America are confused on the gospel, or have syncretized non-biblical belief systems with the message.

- We avoid terminology that does not have good biblical basis. Frequently, phrases are used to express salvation that are not found in the Bible. We feel it is best to use terminology that is consistent with Scripture.

- Since the biblical word "gospel" has taken on baggage not connected to Scripture, with unbelievers we refer to the TERM message as the "Bible's message" rather than the gospel. We have found that the word "gospel" can turn people away as they have a wrong understanding of the word.

- We build a biblical framework for expressing "gospel" truths. In teaching each lesson, the teacher rehearses in his or her mind the Four Irreducible Minimums of the Gospel, and works hard to accurately communicate those parts of the lesson. For example, if one is teaching the Ten Commandments, the emphasis will be on God's holiness and man's helpless, sinful condition. Whenever students think of the "Law," their minds should immediately travel to those two facts. The right lesson focus will help avoid theological muddiness.

- If teaching a mixed group of believers and unbelievers, we draw a line in our minds between *Salvation* and *Sanctification*. TERM has to do with salvation. If we begin to drift off into sanctificational truths, unbelievers will conclude that to "walk with God" and to "get saved" means doing some sort of works. This is critical to understand. You MUST stay with the subject of salvation. You can guarantee confusion if the two are mingled in your presentation.

In teaching on this subject, one of our GOODSEED staff members, Paul Humphreys, has expressed the need to paint a white line down the middle of every church, from the pulpit to the back door. When the pastor teaches on salvation he is to stand on one side of the line, but when he touches on sanctification, he is to move to the other side. In this way the congregation will know not to mix the two truths. I'm sure Paul would settle for an imaginary white line, if every Bible teacher would remember that when he crosses the line without clarification, he will often create confusion. In TERM we stay on the salvation side of the line.

…we need to paint a white line down the middle of every church, from the **pulpit to the back door**.

- A person doesn't need to be a theological wizard to present TERM, but at the same time, any fogginess on the part of the teacher is guaranteed to create an exponential cloud in the mind of students, effectively "hiding" the message from their understanding. When it comes to the message of the gospel, this is a sobering challenge. As teachers, we need to be crystal clear on our message. Our experience has revealed that it is not uncommon for church leaders to be accurate in their understanding of many aspects of the Word, but foggy on what *does* and *does not* constitute the gospel. There is a subtle tendency to blur the message with "add-ons." It takes a mature man to humble himself and seek to be schooled on accuracy. Pastor Dennis Rokser, a successful North American church planter says, *"Fog in the pulpit equals a cloud in the pew."*

Comprehension: We want students to hear and understand the message without any fuzziness, additions or deletions.

- This means tailoring the course for those involved. You will find teaching ESL (English as a Second Language) students a different dynamic than teaching those whose native tongue is English.

- It means moving ahead only as each building block is understood. Don't miss this point. It is folly to proceed on to new material if the present content is still fuzzy. Now in saying this, we have found that people tend to understand each lesson quite well as they are given the information in bite-size pieces.

- Sticking to the progression of the story is critical. One cannot jump ahead. Stick tenaciously to the historical context. If you are introducing the Tabernacle, avoid the temptation to jump ahead and bring Christ into the picture.

- Questions are answered only if they pertain to the present content. Questions having to do with other subject matter are deferred till the end of the study. In TERM, we train teachers how to handle questions in a non-offensive, non-threatening manner.

- Successful communication has occurred when students are able to demonstrate their understanding by clearly articulating, either orally or in writing, the core essentials of what they have been taught. We find that it is critical for the teacher to quiz students on their understanding of the gospel. This is an absolute must. To leave a student fuzzy on the gospel when one could have clarified it with a few simple questions, is spiritual malpractice.

To leave a student **fuzzy** on the gospel when one could have **clarified** things with a few simple questions is spiritual malpractice.

Retention: It is no use learning something if you cannot retain it. We use an approach to learning that scores high on retention.

- We use a "read and see" format rather than a lecture format.

- We encourage the use of visual aids upon which to "hang" concepts. In certain situations, these visual aids are mandatory. But in others cases, one can do fine without them. More on this later.

- Student participation is constant at the level they feel able.

Objectivity: In TERM, we let the message speak for itself. Although a personal testimony given at the appropriate time can have a powerful impact, we must remember that "experience" does not save. Only faith in God's provision brings salvation. To have faith, one must understand the facts. If we promote *experience* over the *facts*, there is great danger that students will put confidence in their experience rather than faith in what Christ has done. It's not that a personal testimony is wrong, it's just that we don't build TERM teaching around it.

- In TERM, we avoid either giving or soliciting statements on how the content of a lesson is impacting a person. In using phrases such as, *"Isn't that wonderful!?"*, we are inviting the students to agree with us. What if they disagree? Worse, they may agree outwardly but disagree inwardly.

In the same way, it is best to avoid open-ended questions. (*"Well, what do you think?"*) Questions should be specific and objective. (*"Do you understand what that paragraph is saying?"*)

- We promote respect by giving students room to make up their own minds. At the same time, we are conscious that the Holy Spirit is doing His work of convicting, putting on pressure in ways we could never imagine.

- A student's questions are handled in such a way that the answer does not overtly focus attention on the one asking the question. Questions on areas that are not part of the immediate content are written down, and the student is informed that they will be answered later after the TERM overview is completed.

- We avoid a subjective presentation that inappropriately pressures students to agree or disagree. We want their responses to be directly related to their understanding of the Word of God. Subjectivity can come in many forms:

   a) **Music:** We can sing *"Just as I am,"* but we need to remember that most unbelievers do not know *"just what they are."* In this day and age of self-esteem and positive-reinforcement, there is a good chance they will not understand their utterly sinful position before a holy God.

   Music certainly has its place in a Christian's life, but to use it to help an unbeliever *decide for Christ* has its risks. We are not saying that to use music is absolutely wrong (the Bible does not forbid it), but a person coming to salvation influenced by a heart-warming refrain can later be persuaded by the Devil or man that his salvation experience was an emotional decision swayed by harmonies and lyrics. In contrast, a person coming to the Lord, basing his faith on an objective, clear presentation of the Scriptures, is almost unmovable. His feet of faith are securely cemented in biblical facts.

We do recognize that many folk are "saved" in situations where a hymn is used to motivate them. May I offer a gentle caution. Remember that a person will only be found "standing on the promises" if he *knows* the promises. We must not neglect a clear, unhurried presentation of the gospel facts.

b) **Invitations:** We can create pressure in unbelievers to respond even though they may not know *what* they are responding to. We must remember that pressure and conviction are two different things. Sales people can master the art of pressure, conning people into buying something they neither want nor need. On the other hand, conviction comes from the Holy Spirit and is directly related to a person understanding the meaning (dunamis) of the Word of God.

c) **Statements:** Statements that contain a rebuke or a challenge must be done carefully. Scripture does contain such examples (Jesus did it), but as a normative approach to communicating the gospel, we find that this is an exception rather than a rule. In teaching TERM, we endeavour to avoid such statements, using a challenge only as a last resort after a clear understanding of the message has occurred and obviously been rejected.

Transferability: Success without a successor is some form of failure. What we teach should also be transferable by our students to others. We want the students to be able to pass on what they have learned.

- This means our approach to teaching must be simple enough for a new believer to imitate. It has been proven that "as you are taught, so you will teach."

- It also means that there must be a way for the teacher to remember all the information that must be communicated.

- The method of teaching must provide for a way to maintain accuracy, objectivity and retention.

> **Success** without a **successor**
> is some form of **failure**

In light of the above, emphasis is not on "oratory" but labours on the practical. We teach in such a way that a "non-teacher" learns to pass on the message. In a real sense, TERM teaching does not teach a gifted communicator how to communicate, but it does teach a gifted teacher a way to teach that can be imitated by someone who is not gifted. The end result is that the success of the teacher is not measured by ability but rather by the content communicated. It is a reliance more on the living Word of God and less on technique.

SUMMARY

We started out by saying that this approach to teaching was seemingly a new way to learn the Scriptures. Actually it is not. Teachers employing this method are found in the early pages of Scripture using it as a means to communicate truth. And no less a person than Jesus used it en route to Emmaus. Thus the reason for calling it THE EMMAUS ROAD MESSAGE.

[1] This is the doctrine of justification. It could be legitimately argued that if one understands the substitutionary work of Christ, then that is sufficient knowledge for salvation. If the person believes, God will impute righteousness even if that person does not know that it has happened.

[2] Teaching chronologically might best be contrasted to topical teaching. Both approaches to teaching are used in the Scripture. The Epistles are examples of topical teaching. Topical teaching is used in the Scripture to correct error and deepen a person's understanding of a specific truth.

[3] Based on this principle, if I only have a few minutes to "witness" to a person, I seek to make sure he understands who God is, and that he is accountable to Him in all his holiness. My initial emphasis is on his lost condition. Invariably I use several of the Ten Commandments in this process. Once again, we must remember that only a lost person knows he needs to be saved.

[4] These goals cannot be universally applied to every evangelistic situation, but many do have a wider application than just TERM.

On DVD—Two Lectures by John R. Cross

What's in a Name: Universally, children are taught, "Never trust a stranger!" And yet, even though many people know virtually nothing about the Lord Jesus, we tell them they need to put their faith in Him.

"What's in a Name" takes a look at two aspects of communication an ambassador must have in mind when introducing a person to the Saviour.

Flying Truth in Formation: We live in a day where the Bible is severely criticized. The prevailing wisdom states "It's impossible to know it's true!"

Not so! The architecture of Scripture is different than any other "sacred" body of literature. Embedded in the very fabric of the Bible is a self-authenticating system that builds a powerful case for the truthfulness of the Word of God.

"Flying Truth in Formation" explores that architecture and explains how Bible believers can confront both a skeptical world and a questioning church with confidence.

CHAPTER 3

understanding the tools

If you have never been exposed to THE EMMAUS ROAD MESSAGE (TERM) before, the best way to become acquainted is to watch a video. A picture is worth a thousand words, and that certainly applies here.

We would suggest you begin by watching either **EE-TAOW!** or **The Taliabo Story**, both videos produced by New Tribes Mission. Either one will give you a quick overview of TERM teaching in a tribal setting.

From there you might wish to watch the sequels to the above videos, although by this time you will have the general idea in mind.

EE-TAOW! *26 min* * Angel Award

EE-TAOW!—The Next Chapter *32 min* * Angel Award

The Taliabo Story *35 min*
* Crown Award—Best film under $100,000
* Angel Award
* Communicator Award of Excellence—Cultural
* Videographer Award of Excellence—Cultural

Delivered from the Power of Darkness *36 min*
* Crown Award—Best Adult Curriculum
* Angel Award
* Communicator Award—Religious Issues
* Videographer Award—Documentary

There is one last video that is worth considering, produced by NTM: **Now We See Clearly** *30 min*

This video illustrates the problem of syncretism and shows how clear teaching made the difference in the understanding of one tribe.

Appealing to the "toolbox" idea again, we will now move on to the tools themselves. It is important to gain an understanding of each TERM product and how to use it.

THE STRANGER ON THE ROAD TO EMMAUS

This fully illustrated, 304-page book is geared for teenagers and adults who know little or nothing about the Bible. It was written for individuals from a western culture, that have been directly or indirectly influenced by Protestant or Catholic beliefs.

THE STRANGER follows the classic TERM approach, beginning in Genesis and moving sequentially through key Old and New Testament stories—from Creation to the Cross. Once you understand how the first tool is assembled, all the other ones will be easy to follow.

The scale on the next page indicates the critical nature of the material as you read through the book. For example, you can teach all the way through THE STRANGER up to Chapter Thirteen and still miss the message if you stop there. Chapter Fourteen is critical and is only correctly understood if the rest of the book has been read sequentially from Chapters One to Thirteen. Chapter Fourteen is what ties everything together. Everything else is "Foundational" content preparing a person for understanding the "Tie Together."

Actually, each chapter is an important building block in developing a scriptural world view in the reader, but it is in Chapter Fourteen that all the threads of previous chapters are brought together to weave a complete mosaic of truth.

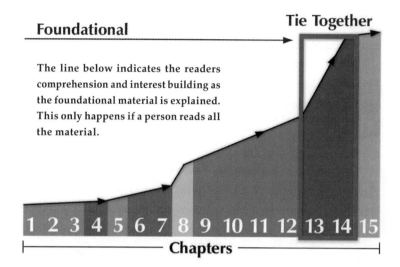

Foundational

Tie Together

The line below indicates the readers comprehension and interest building as the foundational material is explained. This only happens if a person reads all the material.

1 2 3 4 5 6 7 8 9 10 11 12 13 14 15

Chapters

Chapters 1 to 3 The Bible, Attributes of God—Student is excited about his or her new-found knowledge of the Bible and the fact that what has been studied makes sense.

Chapter 4 Fall of Satan and Man, Consequences of Sin—If a student is inclined to quit, it may occur at this point.

Chapter 5 Man's Dilemma, Introduction to Faith, Atonement & Substitution, Noah, Babel—A critical chapter, especially sections one and two. The section on the Flood is hard to teach. It is common for the teacher to lose momentum at the story of Noah. If you know someone who unsuccessfully tried to teach the chronological materials, the chapter on Noah is where he or she most likely gave up. Don't quit.

Chapters 6 to 7 Substitution and Faith again—Student begins to see patterns developing. Teacher finds the going much easier.

Chapter 8 **The Ten Commandments**—A critical chapter. Student will probably grow very quiet while you are teaching. At this point, some ask for a solution to their sin problem. Student may begin to request that the study speed be increased.

Chapters 9 to 12 **The Tabernacle, the Messiah and His life**—Student will be very interested, usually exhibiting an urgency to get to the end of the story.

Chapter 13 **Death, Burial, Resurrection**—Student usually quiet. Material moves along quite quickly.

Chapter 14 **The climax of the story**, where the gospel is presented in the light of all the Scripture. It is at this point that a student may spontaneously share his or her trust in Christ.

Chapter 15 This chapter covers the basics of Sanctification or helps a seeker draw conclusions about the gospel.

Dawn's Story

Dawn was raised in a Christian home in Saskatchewan, Canada. She went to church every Sunday morning and evening and attended the church's kids club and youth group. She even went to a Christian high school. But she wasn't a Christian.

"I just never understood the Bible growing up," she says. "I went through the motions at church, but I didn't have a relationship with God. He just seemed so 'out there' and unreal to me. Honestly, if you had asked me where I was going if I died, I wouldn't have had an answer."

A few years ago, Dawn was working in Alberta and attending a local church, but still felt empty inside. She was searching for something deeper, something to quench her constant thirst. One day, she received the book The Stranger on the Road to Emmaus from a "secret sister" at the church.

As she started reading, her eyes were opened.

"It was as if I was in a dark room and the lights went on. Chapter by chapter, I said to myself, oh, wow! The more I read, the more I understood. I started to understand the animal sacrifices in the Old Testament. I was also finally able to understand why Jesus came, and why he had to be perfect to die. It just made sense. I wondered: How could people not believe this? It was amazing.

"I remember the part that caught my attention most. Right before the crucifixion, Jesus was praying in Gethsemane and he addressed God 'Abba, Father.' When I read that Abba meant daddy, I pictured in my mind God being a father. I thought of my earthly father. I thought how great it was that God, my father, came to earth and died for my sins. I cried when I read that part. It was then that God became real to me and I felt I could have a relationship with Him.

"After I finished reading THE STRANGER, I understood the Bible's message. I was sure of where I was going after I died. I had a real relationship with God."

THE STRANGER WORKBOOK

For those of us who have taught THE STRANGER both with and without the WORKBOOK, there is a unanimous feeling that teaching the material using the WORKBOOK is the only way to go. With the WORKBOOK you are able to review the material in the student's mind. Some of the wrong answers are exactly the sort of answers that you would expect from nominal Christians. Invariably, if something was not clear, it will come out in the process of answering the questions.

The questions in the WORKBOOK should not be viewed as an exam or test. They are review questions only—to help a person make sure they have a grip on the key points. The questions may seem highly simplistic to someone who has a background in the Bible, but experience has shown us that this is just what is needed for beginners.

(For Teens or Adults, Coil-bound, 127 pages, includes answers)

The WORKBOOK can be used in a couple of different ways:

1) **As homework:** This is the preferred method. Leave all WORKBOOK questions for the students to complete on their own at home. This will cause them to think through the material a second time while doing the questions. When you meet again, then review the answers to make sure they are correct. This will be the third time the material has been covered. We have found this to be very effective.

2) **Include it in class time:** During the teaching session, stop at the end of every section and answer the questions at that

point. It will only take a few minutes to complete the quiz and then check the answers. I would use this option if:

a) The student will not be able to do the **WorkBook** homework on his or her own time. Doing the **WorkBook** during class time will add another 3 to 5 hours to your overall study time.

b) The student seems to have problems comprehending each lesson as you progress (not a very common problem). The **WorkBook** will be a double-check before you move on to new material.

c) You are teaching a person who speaks English as a second language. In this case it is important to use the **WorkBook** to insure that the material is being fully understood.

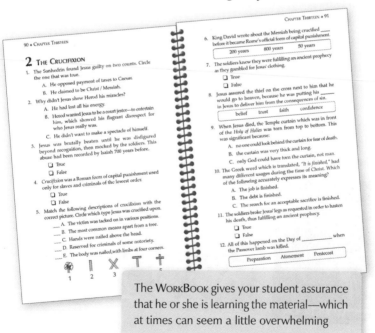

CHAPTER THIRTEEN ◆ 91

90 ◆ CHAPTER THIRTEEN

2 THE CRUCIFIXION

1. The Sanhedrin found Jesus guilty on two counts. Circle the one that was true.
   A. He opposed payment of taxes to Caesar.
   B. He claimed to be Christ / Messiah.

2. Why didn't Jesus show Herod his miracles?
   A. He had lost all his energy.
   B. Herod wanted Jesus to be a court jester—to entertain him, which showed his flagrant disrespect for who Jesus really was.
   C. He didn't want to make a spectacle of himself.

3. Jesus was brutally beaten until he was disfigured beyond recognition, then mocked by the soldiers. This abuse had been recorded by Isaiah 700 years before.
   ❏ True
   ❏ False

4. Crucifixion was a Roman form of capital punishment used only for slaves and criminals of the lowest order.
   ❏ True
   ❏ False

5. Match the following descriptions of crucifixion with the correct picture. Circle which type Jesus was crucified upon.
   ___ A. The victim was tacked on in various positions.
   ___ B. The most common means apart from a tree.
   ___ C. Hands were nailed above the head.
   ___ D. Reserved for criminals of some notoriety.
   ___ E. The body was nailed,with limbs at four corners.

6. King David wrote about the Messiah being crucified ____ before it became Rome's official form of capital punishment.
   | 200 years | 800 years | 50 years |

7. The soldiers knew they were fulfilling an ancient prophecy as they gambled for Jesus' clothing.
   ❏ True
   ❏ False

8. Jesus assured the thief on the cross next to him that he would go to heaven, because he was putting his ____ in Jesus to deliver him from the consequences of sin.
   | belief | trust | faith | confidence |

9. When Jesus died, the Temple curtain which was in front of the Holy of Holies was torn from top to bottom. This was significant because:
   A. no one could look behind the curtain for fear of death.
   B. the curtain was very thick and long.
   C. only God could have torn the curtain, not man.

10. The Greek word which is translated, "It is finished," had many different usages during the time of Christ. Which of the following accurately expresses its meaning?
    A. The job is finished.
    B. The debt is finished.
    C. The search for an acceptable sacrifice is finished.

11. The soldiers broke Jesus' legs as requested in order to hasten his death, thus fulfilling an ancient prophecy.
    ❏ True
    ❏ False

12. All of this happened on the Day of ____ when the Passover lamb was killed.
    | Preparation | Atonement | Pentecost |

The **WorkBook** gives your student assurance that he or she is learning the material—which at times can seem a little overwhelming

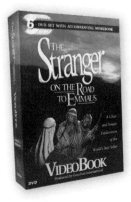

THE STRANGER VIDEOBOOK
Award Winning Series

This award winning DVD is an eleven-hour series that clearly and logically explains the gospel, from Creation to the Cross. Following THE STRANGER ON THE ROAD TO EMMAUS book, often word for word, the greatest of stories is brought to life on screen.

Using over 70 visual aids, John Cross leads the viewer through the gospel story in a way that is unforgettable. This is one DVD series you will want for your own use—and for lending or giving away!

SUGGESTIONS ON USING THE DVD

The six DVD's are packaged in a box along with one WORKBOOK. This package design facilitates passing the product on to an individual with the idea of being "ready to go." For two or more people additional WORKBOOKS would be needed. It

— Excellent —
Give to a Friend
Small Groups
Camps
Weekend Retreats
Sunday Schools
Home Schoolers
Christian Schools

is important that each viewer have a WORKBOOK. For larger groups, there are discounts on bulk orders.

Includes the 6 DVD set plus a WORKBOOK

It is important to understand that this DVD series is different than any other "Bible Study" in which you may have participated. This series is really ONE story and ONE story only. If you do not finish the series, it will have been like building a house, but not putting up walls or completing the roof. The first 13 chapters are foundational, with the 14th chapter tying everything together into a powerful presentation of the gospel. But to understand the 14th chapter, you need the foundations found in the preceding 13 chapters. Treat this series as one story.

In light of the above, it is best to watch the series in as short a time as possible. This can easily be done in one or two weeks if only a few people are watching it together. For larger groups, a weekend "retreat" is ideal. With a little advance planning, it can also be spread over a number of weeks. See the suggested schedules on pages 60 & 61 to help budget your time. Once again, remember, don't drag the series out over such a long time that the ONE story begins to fragment in listeners' minds.

The entire series is approximately eleven hours in length and is divided into 52 sections with each section running between 4 to 27 minutes. You can watch as many or as few sections as you like in any given sitting.

Lectures are in classroom and on location

There are 15 chapters in the series, some very short and others quite long. It does not work to view them according to chapters. Instead view it by sections. If you have an hour, you will be able to watch several sections in that time. Its as easy as 1,2,3,4:

1. To begin, insert the first DVD in your player, sit down and watch the first section (actually sections 1 & 2). It will take nine minutes.

2. At the end of the section, the on-screen hosts will ask you to put the DVD on "pause" and complete the questions found in the accompanying WORKBOOK. Completing the WORKBOOK takes only a few minutes and is very helpful in anchoring the key points. We strongly recommend the use of the WORKBOOK. Comprehension and retention are significantly higher among those who do.

The DVD chart on the next two pages is based on actual DVD viewing and **WorkBook** time. Prayer time, songs and breaks for snacks would be in addition to this time.

From the chart you can see that if you meet once a week and you plan your actual study time to be 75 minutes, then it will take you 15 weeks to go through the six DVD's. For home studies, we recommend 75 minute sessions, twice a week, over a period of 8 weeks.

3. After the questions have been completed, check the back of the **WorkBook** for the answers. Review any questions that were answered incorrectly to make sure all the content has been understood. (NOTE: At this point it would be helpful to have the full text of the DVD series, which is the book, **The Stranger on the Road to Emmaus**).

4. Once the **WorkBook** is completed—it will take only a few minutes—push "play" on the DVD and view the next section.

In this way you progress through the entire series. The total time needed to play the DVD series and complete the **WorkBook** will differ for each person or group.

Chapter	Section	120 Min Sessions	90 Min Sessions	75 Min Sessions	60 Min Sessions	DVD Disk
One	1. Prologue — 1 min					
	2. Getting Things Straight — 8 min				Session 1	
	3. A Unique Book — 16 min		Session 1	Session 1		DVD 1
Two	1. In the Beginning God — 12 min	Session 1				
	2. Angels, Hosts and Stars — 9 min				Session 2	
Three	1. Heaven and Earth — 10 min					
	2. It Was Good — 20 min		Session 2	Session 2		
	3. Man and Woman — 18 min				Sess 3	
Four	1. I Will — 10 min					
	2. Has God said? — 18 min	Session 2			Sess 4	
	3. Where are you? — 11 min		Session 3	Session 3		
	4. Death — 18 min				Sess 5	DVD 2
Five	1. A Paradox — 16 min					
	2. Atonement — 25 min	Session 3		Sess 4	Session 6	
	3. Two by Two — 27 min		Session 4			
	4. Babel — 8 min			Session 5		
Six	1. Abraham — 9 min				Session 7	
	2. Belief — 6 min		Session 5			
	3. Isaac — 14 min	Session 4				
Seven	1. Israel and Judah — 4 min			Session 6		DVD 3
	2. Moses — 8 min		Session 6		Session 8	
	3. Pharaoh and the Passover — 16 min					
Eight	1. Bread, Quail and Water — 7 min			Session 7		
	2. Ten Rules — 18 min				Sess 9	
	3. The Courtroom — 15 min					
Nine	1. The Tabernacle — 21 min	Session 5	Session 7	Session 8	Session 10	DVD 4

Sessions are timed to allow for WorkBook review.

Chapter	Section		120 Min Sessions	90 Min Sessions	75 Min Sessions	60 Min Sessions	DVD Disk
Nine	1a. The Gold Box*	12 min	Sess 5	Session 7	Sess 8	10	DVD 4
	2. Unbelief	10 min				Session 11	
	3. Judges, Kings and Prophets	14 min			Session 9		
Ten	1. Elizabeth, Mary and John	14 min	Session 6	Session 8		Session 12	
	2. Jesus	15 min			Session 10		
	3. Among the Sages	8 min					
	4. Baptism	12 min					
Eleven	1. Tempted	11 min		Session 9		Session 13	DVD 5
	2. Power and Fame	7 min			Session 11		
	3. Nicodemus	10 min					
	4. Rejection	11 min					
	5. The Bread of Life	7 min				Session 14	
Twelve	1. Filthy Rags	8 min	Session 7				
	2. The Way	4 min					
	3. Lazarus	10 min		Session 10			
	4. Hell	6 min			Session 12		
	5. Acceptance and Betrayal	7 min					
Thirteen	1. The Arrest	9 min	Session 8			Session 15	
	2. The Crucifixion	27 min					
	3. The Burial and Resurrection	14 min		Session 11	Session 13		
Fourteen	1. The Stranger	8 min				Session 16	DVD 6
	2. TERM - Adam to Noah	18 min	Session 9				
	3. TERM - Abraham to the Law	25 min		Sess 12	Sess 14	17	
	4. TERM - Tab to Brazen Serpent	23 min				18	
	5. TERM - John to Resurrection	22 min		Sess 13	Sess 15	19	
Fifteen	1. A Convenient Time**	12 min					

* This DVD lesson is highly visual and almost impossible to explain in written form. For this reason it is not found in "THE STRANGER" book.

** At this point the DVD series differs from "THE STRANGER" book.

AWARDS FOR EXCELLENCE

TELLY SILVER
Live Events

TELLY SILVER
Use of Animation

THE COMMUNICATOR
Award of Excellence: Educational

THE COMMUNICATOR
Award of Excellence: Videography

ANGEL AWARD
Excellence in Media

CROWN AWARD
Adult Curriculum

A LEARNING EXPERIENCE

My preference for preparing to teach the TERM study in my home was to participate in a TERM seminar. Unfortunately, scheduling and travel were limiting factors. I was excited when I received my copy of THE STRANGER ON THE ROAD TO EMMAUS VIDEOBOOK and discovered that this wonderful presentation of THE EMMAUS ROAD MESSAGE is both a learning and teaching tool.

I used the VIDEOBOOK to pace myself through the study of each section of the textbook while taking note of presentation style, use of visual aids, and flow of the study. In certain sections of the study, I used the VIDEOBOOK to show the students a few of the more complex visual aids, special animated graphics and footage shot on location in Biblical lands. At the completion of the study, feedback from the students was that the textbook, workbook, and multiple media sources helped broaden and enhance their learning experience.

THE STRANGER CORRESPONDENCE COURSE

This specially-adapted WorkBook is designed to be used with The Stranger at "a distance"—a way some prefer to get acquainted with the Bible.

The questions are divided by chapter and are formatted for ease of correcting. Perforations allow for easy removal of the completed sections and to facilitate mailing. The Teacher's Answer Book takes the work out of correcting the lessons.

- Prison Ministries will appreciate the flexibility offered by this course. If an inmate is moved, the course can "go-along," allowing for the study to continue. Unlike the WorkBook, the Correspondence Course is not coil-bound, allowing for easier access to prisons.

- Missions, Radio & TV ministries or anyone reaching out to people isolated from others, will find this tool useful in teaching the Bible.

- Pastors & Youth Workers wishing to sponsor correspondence ministries from their local churches, can reach those in their congregations of whom they are unsure regarding salvation. These folks are often adherents who sneak into the pew now and then but don't want "special attention." They may agree to a study of the Bible in private, opening a door to follow their progress at a distance. This is also an excellent way to strengthen individuals who are weak in Bible basics.

THE STRANGER AUDIOBOOK

The AUDIOBOOK is a professionally-mastered production of the second edition of THE STRANGER. Randy Zempel reads the commentary and Therese Gruba gives life to the Scriptures as they lend their professional voices to a clear presentation of the gospel message.

The AUDIOBOOK has found a niche with the seeing impaired, professional drivers who tend to "read" a lot on the road, and those who prefer listening rather than reading. We have heard stories of those who listen to this series over and over again.

Available in:
  English (Cassettes, CDs & MP)
  Spanish (CDs & MP3)

Listening to the Story

I must confess that I am not a "born reader." I do appreciate listening to a story especially if it is interesting or helpful. I can still recall listening to a dramatic story on my Dad's old radio as a child. I had a similar experience when I first listened to THE STRANGER audio book on my car stereo. It was compelling, clear and easy to listen to.

By the time I had reached the end of the book Randy Zempel and Terese Gruba had become good companions and friends on my journeys. My understanding of the Bible had also been greatly enhanced even though I had been a student of the Bible for many years.

The Bible was not only more understandable but the God of the Bible was more real to me and I felt I knew Him at a deeper level than I had previously grasped. Like the two disciples I now have a burning heart and a burning desire to share this story with others.

THE STRANGER ON THE ROAD TO EMMAUS

CHINESE:
Traditional Script &
Simplified Script

FRENCH

FRENCH
WORKBOOK

GERMAN

PORTUGUESE

PORTUGUESE
WORKBOOK

RUSSIAN

SPANISH

KOREAN

ALL THAT THE PROPHETS HAVE SPOKEN

ALL THE PROPHETS (ATP) is written using the same approach you find in THE STRANGER, but adapted for those who have had significant exposure to Islam. The two books are about 25% different, but those differences are important.

Islam is said to be the fastest growing religion in the world. For the first time, many Christians are meeting Muslims as immigrants pour into Europe and North America. Muslims, disengaged from family and religion, tend to be curious. While most would never admit it, many are searching for something more. The violence of Muslim extremists coupled with the severe policies of some Islamic states, have created disillusionment.

Muslims are commanded by their holy book—the Qur'an—to believe the Torah of Moses, the Psalms of David and the Gospel of Jesus. The Qur'an refers regularly to some twenty Bible prophets. Because of this, Muslims will often tell you that they "believe all the prophets!" But even a cursory reading of the Qur'an reveals that Islam rejects Jesus as the crucified Son of God! In reality they don't believe the prophets at all.

The printed page is a powerful tool for reaching folks entrenched in Islam. Most Muslims will never risk attending a Christian meeting, but they will observe the lives of Christians, listen to radio programs and read literature. ALL THE PROPHETS is a tool for directing Muslims to the One of whom all the prophets bore witness.

Chapters 1 to 3 Briefly explains how the Bible has not been changed. Couch the attributes of God in his "greatness." (ex. God is great because he is eternal. God is great becuase he is all-powerful. God is great because ... , etc.) Muslims believe God is great, but not as great as the scripture reveals.

Chapter 4 Fall of Satan and Man, Consequences of Sin. Sin is not a "big deal" to Muslims, but as God is lifted up in his greatness, the sin of man becomes an issue.

Chapter 5 Man's Dilemma, Atonement & Substitution, The Prophet Enoch, The Prophet Noah, the story of Babel.

Chapters 6 to 7 Faith is introduced with the Prophet Abraham. The Bible's perspective on Ishmael and Isaac is presented. The concept of substitution is continued with the Passover.

Chapter 8 The Ten Commandments – A critical chapter. The "sin problem" is now looming large.

Chapters 9 to 12 The Tabernacle, the Messiah and His life. The true identity of Jesus is slowly revealed from scripture. Time is taken to address issues surrounding the Trinity.

Chapter 13 Death, Burial, Resurrection. Yes, it was Jesus on the cross and he really did die. He also rose again.

Chapter 14 The climax of the story, where the gospel is presented in the light of all the Scripture. The identity of Jesus is made clear, as well as the reason for his death and resurrection.

Chapter 15 The question one must answer, "Do you believe all that the prophets have spoken?"

ALL THAT THE PROPHETS HAVE SPOKEN

ARABIC   **FRENCH**   **TURKISH**

...it will have great impact on the people who read it. I can say that because I live with 98% Moslems and this book would open their eyes. It is so clear and easy to understand. ...It is going to be helpful to the Moslems and the Jews to understand the reason that Jesus had to come to earth.   **an email from Bethlehem**

Also available as a CORRESPONDENCE COURSE

ENGLISH & FRENCH

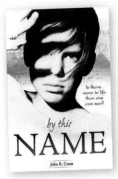

BY THIS NAME

BY THIS NAME is a very different book than THE STRANGER. It assumes total Bible illiteracy—that the person knows nothing of Scripture! It was written for those coming from cultures heavily influenced by polytheistic, pantheistic, and animistic belief systems—religions historically found in the east or in tribal cultures. They worshiped many gods, ancestral spirits, or atheistic philosophies. But now with the rise of post-modernism, the wide acceptance of various psychologies, and the popularity of the New Age, that form of thinking permeates much of the western world.

This book helps explain the Bible, not only to Hindus, Shintos, Buddhists, ancestral worshipers and animists, but also to New Agers, post-moderns, secularists, Mormons, Jehovah Witnesses, and Christian Scientists.

"Westerners" have become very panthistic in their view of God. A 2003 Ipos-Reid survey revealed the following about how Canadians percieve God.

   77% Impersonal spiritual force
   17% A person
   87% Present in all of nature
   76% Present in every human being

"We'll be viewing God as something akin to 'the force' in the movie Star Wars—as an energy, a consciousness, rather than a person..."

Robert Fuller, professor of religious studies Bradley University, Peoria, Ill.

Reader's Digest Nov 2003

Chapters 1 to 3   The polytheist has problems with the first four words of the Bible. They don't believe in a "beginning"—they believe in the circle of life. And when you say the word "God" they want to know which god out of several million. If you say the Creator God, they will think of their creator god, not the Creator of the Bible. For this reason we start BY THIS NAME with establishing a name for God, (he is called Yahweh), and the fact that Yahweh is unique or holy. (The identity of other gods is left open, and their existence is not denied.) Beginning with creation, we start to learn about Yahweh. Special attention is given to the Creator-creation distinction and the fact that man is made in God's image.

Chapter 4   The origin of evil is discussed, beginning with the fall of Lucifer and extending eventually to mankind. Since "what constitutes sin" is very garbled in eastern religions, the nature of sin is introduced and sin's connection with death is established.

Chapter 5   Adam & Eve, Cain & Abel, Noah, Babel—Since eastern religions believe in many ways to God, "two ways" to God are introduced, with only one being acceptable. This theme is carried on throughout the book, with each wrong way being examined, and the right way being affirmed. Since the eastern religions are very sensitive to "blood," the sacrificial system is introduced with minimal details, leaving further information to later.

Chapters 6 to 7   Faith is introduced with Abraham. The concept of substitution is continued with the Passover. The history of Yahweh as a reliable and faithful God is building.

Chapter 8   The Ten Commandments—The nature of sin is nailed down, and the identity of the "other" gods is unmasked. From this point on idolatry is openly and aggressively addressed.

Chapters 9 to 12 The Tabernacle, True versus False Prophets, the identity of the Messiah (He is Yahweh) His life, the nature of the Trinity—issues all examined.

Chapter 13 Death, Burial, Resurrection—not a reincarnation.

Chapter 14 The climax of the story, where the person and work of Christ is presented in the light of all the Scripture.

Chapter 15 Covers the basics of Sanctification and discusses the importance of not delaying a decision to trust in Christ.

Clothed in His Righteousness

"Every day, people ask me questions about the Bible, and I don't know how to answer them," said the young school teacher. She lived in Nagaland, a northeast Indian province characterized by nominal Christianity practiced alongside tribal animism. "One of the most frequently asked questions is: If I am a Christian and sin, am I still saved? Can I still go to heaven? Even I myself was confused about sin."

Her confusions dissipated after attending a GOODSEED TERM seminar held in her region in January 2006. Like many others who attended the seminar, she came away rejoicing in her salvation after gaining a fresh understanding of Christ's work on the cross.

"The visual aid using the cloaks showed me that God has clothed me with his righteousness. Even though I sin, I am still accepted before God in heaven!" she said excitedly, stretching out her arm and pointing heavenward. "This gives me great joy."

Another man was impressed by the same visual aid that pictured justification before God. He said: "I now understand that Christ's righteousness covers me. I don't have to focus on my own shortcomings anymore! I am very happy and I want to praise God."

THE WAY OF RIGHTEOUSNESS

Paul Bramsen, a missionary for many years in Africa, adapted the TERM outline for radio. Though this 543-page book was written for an African-Muslim audience, it has far wider applications. The preface says it all.

Preface:"*Even if a log soaks a long time in water, it will never become a crocodile*" (Wolof proverb)…nor does being religious make a person righteous. Religious rituals and good deeds may make people feel righteous and even appear righteous before men, but they do not make them righteous before God.

THE WAY OF RIGHTEOUSNESS is an English translation of "Yoonu Njub"—a **series of radio-programs** originally written in the Wolof language for the Muslim people of Senegal, West Africa. Beginning with the Torah of Moses, these **one hundred 15-minute lessons** take the listener on a journey through the Scriptures of the prophets to view God's unchangeable purpose for mankind and to hear God's thrilling answer to the prophet Job's four-thousand-year-old question, "*How can a man be righteous before God?*" (Job 9:2)

Muslims believe that God has revealed His will through four sacred books (Torah, Psalms, Gospel, Qur'an). Yet few Muslims ever have the opportunity to hear the Good News of God according to the Torah, the Psalms, and the Gospel Writings.

The reason for making these lessons available in English is twofold:

1. To facilitate translation into other languages for broadcast around the world;

2. To promote reading by English-speaking Muslims and others who want to deepen their understanding of the stories.

Firm Foundations

New Tribes Mission has created a whole spectrum of products built around the "Firm Foundations" theme. Whether called "Firm Foundations" or "TERM" these products are closely related when it comes to the method used in communicating the Scripture. The content does vary depending on the product and for whom it was created.

If you are working with animistic people, then you will want to obtain the series of books entitled, "Building on Firm Foundations." The first volume in the series is a "must read" for anyone interested in this approach to evangelism. It is a classic.

We would encourage you to contact NTM directly for a catalog; (they have regional offices in many countries) or visit their web site at: www.ntm.org

Teacher's Manual
Firm Foundations: Creation to Christ

Designed specifically as a teacher's manual, Firm Foundations is laid out as a Sunday School curriculum, its 50 lessons spread across one year. Effective for both adults and teens, this course works well for a "total church" learning experience when combined with the children's edition. (591 pages)

Firm Foundations: Creation to Christ
Children's Edition

This five-book series is designed for the teacher who is schooling reading-age children. This excellent resource walks you step by step through each lesson. Use it with your Church Sunday School or family.

THE LAMB
PICTUREBOOK & CD

THE LAMB was written for young children, ages 5 through 8. Since being released, we have found it accepted by every age. The elderly especially seem to appreciate the simplicity of the message.

THE LAMB presents the gospel without watering it down or avoiding issues. Subjects such as sin and death are taught in an honest, head-on manner. At the same time, the child is not left hanging. Even the lesson dealing with death ends with hope.

To keep the narrative simple, the central teachings found in the Old Testament are clustered around two people, Adam and Eve. It was felt that to introduce too many Bible characters would unnecessarily complicate the message for little children.

THE LAMB is designed for ten sittings. It is suggested that you, along with your child, listen to a different chapter each night, no less than three times a week. No advance preparation is required—a review is built in at the beginning of each lesson and questions are included at the end. The review is part of the lesson and is recorded on tape. The questions are found in the booklet under the chapter headings. Listening time for each chapter runs four to six minutes.

AVAILABLE IN: **English, French & Spanish**

THE LAMB **is also being used as an ESL (English Second Language) curriculum with adults.**

THE LAMB POWERPOINT

THE LAMB PPT comes with a DVD disc which includes all the pictures found in THE LAMB PICTUREBOOK. We would encourage you to teach the material yourself using the accompanying lesson book, however if you prefer you can use the pre-recorded narration.

The PPT is divided into both five and ten lesson formats, each lesson including optional review questions (pdf files on the disc). If you use the recorded narration, the listening time for each lesson runs four to twelve minutes depending on the format chosen. The review questions usually add another 10 to 20 minutes.

EXCELLENT FOR CHILDREN IN ALL SETTINGS:

- Sunday school
- Children's church
- After-school clubs
- Pastor's "story time for children" before sermon
- Special one-time presentations
- Outreach event
- Home devotions
- Children's camp
- Family camp children's program

THE LAMB DVD: JUST THE STORY

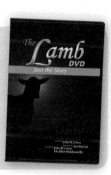

This DVD is built with the illustrations and audio narration that's found in the book, THE LAMB. Told as one continuous story without chapter breaks or review, one can watch the story without interruption.

"I believe, Mr. Joe, I believe!"

Joe had been teaching THE LAMB at Backyard Bible Clubs at the same neighborhood in Georgia every summer for the past four years. Many kids came year after year to hear "Mr. Joe" teach, but this was the first year Tommy showed up.

Ten-year-old Tommy was a challenge from the start. He was full of energy, constantly interrupted, and asked irrelevant questions.

"Hold your questions until later, Tommy," Joe would say. If Tommy got too disruptive for the class of 30 children, Joe would send him to the back to sit with the host. He wasn't sure whether Tommy really understood the teaching or not.

The same thing went on every night. The fifth night—the night of the important wrap up—Tommy sat at the back again.

After teaching on Jesus' death and resurrection, Joe challenged the children: "Do you believe? Do you believe what the Bible tells us? Do you believe that Jesus is your Lamb? Do you believe?"

Joe wasn't expecting a verbal answer, so it surprised him when an excited, young voice called out from the back.

"I BELIEVE! I BELIEVE, Mr. Joe, I BELIEVE!"

Tommy's voice rang out loud and clear. He had understood the message—and he wasn't afraid to make it known!

But Tommy wasn't the only one who got the Bible's message this summer. More than 100 teachers and volunteers reached out to 600 children of all ages when the Atlanta-area church put on Backyard Bible Clubs at homes in 25 different neighborhoods.

Most of the children who came were unchurched.

"We had always done a Vacation Bible School at our church, but I've always wondered why we bring our own kids and teach them what they hear every week," says Joe, who has served in children's ministry for 22 years. "Why not go to the neighborhoods and share THE LAMB with kids who aren't part of our church?"

And not only were children reached with the Gospel, but their families as well. This summer, moms and dads "hung out" to hear the teaching. One Hindu dad videotaped the Bible lessons. Two Buddhist grandparents came and asked questions. They each received the book THE STRANGER ON THE ROAD TO EMMAUS.

"The world is here," the children's ministry director, Denise, says of the diverse metropolitan Atlanta area. "We don't have to get on an airplane to go. It's already here."

Andrea, who hosted a club, reports: "One 7-year-old girl comes from a family where the mom is not a believer. She would share the Bible story with the entire family at dinner every night. She even asked her mom if she had ever heard any of the stories before. I am so excited that God is using the Bible club to bring His Word to this family."

The church encourages the hosts to follow up with the children and their families. In the months that follow, some invite their neighbors to church. Others start Bible studies in their homes. Many continue to answers questions from the children and their families about the Bible and about God.

Bible teacher Joe baptized a girl three years after she attended a club where he taught THE LAMB. "She was one of the kids from the neighborhood who did not have a church home," he says. "After the backyard club, her family started coming to church. We were teaching the fourth- and fifth-graders THE STRANGER when she accepted Christ and asked me to baptize her. Having been involved in her life, it was special for me to witness her understanding the Gospel."

He continues: "I am a huge fan of our backyard Bible clubs, and I believe what makes them most successful is THE LAMB materials that we are using. Kids want the truth taught. They really want to know who God is. The Lamb is so well put together to teach in a short week like this. You never know who you're going to touch with it. It may be the 3- to 4-year-olds; it may be the 17-year-old who helps out; or it may be the dad who comes and asks questions."

Carrie, another volunteer, sums it up this way: "Backyard Bible Clubs is the most outstanding evangelical tool I think I have ever seen!"

TERM Seminar Training

Most of us have to see how something is done before we get a feel for how to go about it ourselves.

A TERM Seminar functions on the principle that "as you are taught, so you will teach." A TERM seminar models the most effective approach to communicating TERM content. Over seventy visual aids are demonstrated. The seminar functions on the principle that "as you are taught, so you will teach."

Specific dates and details are posted at: www.goodseed.com

What will I learn?

Using just such a setting, TERM participants are taught how to lead a small group Bible study using GoodSeed tools. Background information, tips on how to teach, ideas to illustrate points, ways to stay on track, and how to defuse potential problems are all addressed.

The seminar models an approach to teaching that most Christians can imitate successfully.

Can I miss sessions?

Participants are expected to attend the entire seminar. We ask that no audio or video recordings be made of the sessions.

How long is a TERM Seminar?

Teaching time averages 22 hours. A TERM seminar is an intense time of learning with lecture periods averaging 40 to 50 minutes.

Is there any charge for the Seminar?

The cost of the three-day seminar varies. The seminar fees cover lunch, supper, snacks and all materials (the one exception is Ontario, Canada, where meals are not included). Visual aids and other resources for TERM teaching are available for purchase at the seminar.

Who is a typical attendee?

The seminar is designed for believers. We regularly have attendees who consider themselves beginners in sharing their faith. Pastors, as well as home and foreign missionaries have found the seminar highly profitable.

What about lodging?

Lodging is your responsibility. Upon registration, we will provide you with contact information for local motels and bed & breakfasts.

Call us for a registration form or save time with online registration.

www.goodseed.com

EQUIPPING YOU TO SHARE YOUR FAITH!

CHAPTER 4

visual aids

In teaching TERM, we have found visual aids almost indispensable in communicating biblical truth. Of course TERM can be taught without "props", but when possible we do use them.

God himself used many visual aids to teach us things about his person and his work. Psalm 19 tell us that creation itself is like a huge visual aid that declares the glory of God. Jesus, when he walked the earth, referred to vines, flowers and fields to make a point. The altar and the cross are both places associated with death, and for the believer reminders of the substitutionary work of Christ.

There are topics in the Bible that are almost impossible to communicate without a visual. For example, the Tabernacle of Moses is very hard to teach without pictures. And yet the stories surrounding the Tabernacle provides foundational background to the New Testament. Without that background, Jesus' confrontation with the temple priests, the Pharisees and the Sanhedrin do not make sense. The incredible events surrounding the birth of John the Baptist lose all luster. Zechariah's identity as a priest means nothing (was he a Buddhist priest or a Roman Catholic priest?), and his conversation with an angel beside the Altar of Incense lacks context.

For this reason GOODSEED has been working to develop 3-dimensional visual aids, not only of the Tabernacle, but for teaching other areas as well. It is our goal to make all those visuals available to those who desire them.

SCALE: 1 TO 90

THE TABERNACLE MODEL KIT

Bring out the Tabernacle and both children and adults gather around like bees around honey. This model gives a complete overview of the structure. It's ideal for classroom demonstration and one-on-one teaching. It's also an extremely helpful tool in teaching through THE STRANGER.

Parents and teachers assemble the model with their children, painting the pieces as they teach. One Bible College requires all students to assemble their own kit as they write a paper on the Tabernacle.

Allow three hours for assembly, more if painted. A detailed instruction manual is included or can be viewed online, along with, at:

www.goodseed.com

Dimensions: 23" x 12" x 4" (59 x 31 x 10 cm)
Scale: 1 to 90
Weight: 3 lbs (1.4 kg)

Twelve free downloadable Sunday School lessons online!

Scale: 1 to 10
The Tabernacle Furniture

This set of Tabernacle Furniture comes fully assembled. It compliments the usage of the model in that you can show a larger item in your teaching. This is a high quality product. See the next page for more details.

Good for all ages
- VBS & Sunday Schools
- Family & Small Groups
- Home & Christian Schools
- Evangelism & Discipleship
- Camps & Retreats
- Church & Missions
- Colleges & Seminaries

THE TABERNACLE FURNITURE SET

- Scale 1:10 (illustrations not to scale)
- Fully Assembled
- Metal Construction
- Antique Bronze & Gold Electroplated Finish

THE BRAZEN ALTAR

People are often surprised at the size of this altar. It was quite large in comparison to the other pieces. There is debate as to whether the grate was inside the altar across the middle or down along the lower side. We did both, with the inside grate being removable. Both interpetations can be taught.

THE TABLE

We don't know how the bread was placed. We provide loaves as shown, but our website explains how these can be changed.

THE LAVER

Other than the fact it was some sort of water container and it had a base, we have no dimesions for this piece of furniture. We sized ours based on the fact it had to be carried.

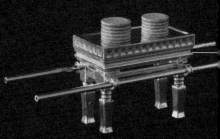

THE LAMPSTAND

Though we know its shape, the Bible does not give the size of the menorah. However, when Titus destroyed the Jewish Temple, he made an Arch in Rome that shows the plundered furniture. We based our design on a careful study of this monument.

THE ARK OF THE COVENANT

The overall instructions for constructing the Ark are quite specific with the exception of the cherubim. We kept the detail simple without losing its beauty. This is an item that can be left on your desk or mantel as a conversation starter. Once you have someone interested you can give them a copy of THE STRANGER or BY THIS NAME. Includes Tablets of the Law, Pot of Manna and Aaron's rod.

THE ALTAR OF INCENSE

Also known as the Golden Altar. One advantage to 3-dimensional visual aids is that they can be handled. All of these pieces are quite robust and should last for years.

common blunders

———————————— ✦ ————————————

- **Taking too long**

  Without doubt, taking too long to complete the TERM study is the most common error in TERM teaching. When the content is stretched out over too many weeks, each lesson begins to stand alone as an independent Bible lesson rather than part of one continuous story. It takes about 12 to 18 hours to teach through THE STRANGER, ALL THE PROPHETS or BY THIS NAME depending on your teaching experience and the number of visual aids that you use. We have found it best to spread those hours over no longer a period than 4 to 6 weeks. To go longer has almost universally proven to be a mistake.

- **Poor expression when reading (monotonous)**

  If you read the lesson with a flat monotone, it won't be long before folks have lost interest. The content must be communicated with genuine expression. The way words, phrases and concepts are emphasized—punched—are all part of showing the significance of what is being taught. To read well you must practice, practice, practice.

- **Jumping ahead of the progression**

  Learn one section at a time in the sequence it is written. This is not the type of Bible study where you can jump around from one lesson to another. For example, after teaching on the Ten Commandments, you may sense that your students are under conviction of sin. They may make comments like, *"I feel so dirty"* or *"I'm in trouble."* You may be tempted to jump ahead and give them the gospel. But wait! Think for a moment. On more than one occasion Jesus had a seeker indicate an openesss to the gospel but Jesus did not "jump ahead."

Now a man came up to Jesus and asked, "Teacher, what good thing must I do to get eternal life?"   Matthew 19:16

Think how you would feel if your next door neighbor asked you that question. It's the "witnessing" opportunity we all dream of having. If you are like me, I would be tempted to immediately launch into an explanation of the gospel … but Jesus didn't do that. Rather he gave the man a good dose of the law.

"Why do you ask me about what is good?" Jesus replied. "There is only One who is good. If you want to enter life, obey the commandments."

"Which ones?" the man inquired.

Jesus replied, "'Do not murder, do not commit adultery, do not steal, do not give false testimony, honor your father and mother,' and 'love your neighbor as yourself.'"

Matthew 19:17-19

If Jesus had been attending many of our schools on evangelism he would have been given a failing grade right then and there. But Jesus knew the young man had no sense of being lost, so he gave him the law. The Bible tells us that the law makes us conscious of our sinfulness. Did it work?

"All these I have kept," the young man said. "What do I still lack?"   Matthew 19:20

The young man still felt he was pretty good. Jesus took it a step further. He interpreted the meaning of the law—the fact that it is centered on God and others, not on self.

> Jesus answered, "If you want to be perfect, go, sell your possessions and give to the poor, and you will have treasure in heaven. Then come, follow me."
>
> When the young man heard this, he went away sad, because he had great wealth.   Matthew 19:21-22

The young man now knew he was far short of God's perfection. Jesus had successfully communicated to him a core issue of the gospel—that is, we are all helpless sinners.

So what's the point? During a pregnancy, a baby is not delivered the first time the mother feels the child kick! In the same way, don't rush the spiritual birth. It takes time to clearly present who Jesus is, and what he did on the cross. Only then will the gospel make sense.

- **Assuming too much**

  Since we have spent quite a bit of time on this subject, I will not go into any more depth. Once again, the WORKBOOK is the best resource to help determine comprehension.

- **Getting off on side issues**

  Since TERM covers Scripture from *Creation to the Ascension of Christ*, there is plenty of content along the way whereby a student can take one off on unrelated subjects. Some students are particularly adept at changing the subject or introducing controversial issues. Believers tend to be the worst culprits. Unbelievers often don't know the questions to ask, and since they find the content quite challenging as it is, they are much more likely to stick to the program. There are two key means for keeping the study on track:

1. The **WorkBook**: This tool is an excellent means for keeping the study focused on the subject at hand.

2. The clothes line illustration (page 7 of **The Stranger**): When you cover this chapter, point out to the student that not all the clothes are being hung on the line—some are still down in the clothes basket. These "other clothes" represent the many questions and subjects that are not covered in TERM. When a person asks a question that belongs in the clothes basket, mention it as such—"That's a clothes basket question", and then offer to write it down and answer it later, AFTER the complete TERM study is done. Once the student has the big picture in mind, you can go back and fill in the details by answering his or her questions.

*   **Losing objectivity**

    A popular approach to Bible Study is to ask everyone present what they think about a particular subject. Usually you end up with a collection of shared ignorance. Once the study is moved to the basis of "my opinion" versus "your opinion" it has lost its direction. What really matters is God's opinion.

    A common place to lose objectivity is in the introduction and conclusion of any session. Opening in prayer makes sense to believers, but for unbelievers it can be intimidating and uncomfortable—they have no one to pray to. Worse yet, some may feel comfortable praying, indicating in their mind that everything is "right" with God. A prayer may give them a false sense of security. (The same could be said of singing.)

I suggest you do your praying before your students arrive, and then just launch into the lesson when they show up.

We would strongly suggest that in a TERM study you take an objective approach to your student's religious world view. To challenge a world view prematurely can create real problems. As you teach, the Scripture itself will expose the wrong way of thinking. Any arguments will be with what the Bible says.

- **Teacher does not determine if student understood content at each building block level**

To continue on without the student understanding each building block is to be a teacher flying on autopilot. The WorkBook is the best resource to check comprehension at each level. It is especially critical that students not miss the content related to the Ten Commandments. People must first know they are lost before they will desire to be saved.

ideas that really work

There are many different ways one can share the gospel using TERM, but let me list some that we have found effective.

- **Give Away:** Give a copy of THE STRANGER book or DVD to a friend, neighbor—anyone who you feel will read or watch it, but for one reason or another will not have the time to join a Bible study. If the person is from a Muslim background or originated from a Muslim country, give him or her a copy of ALL THE PROPHETS. New Ager's, or other eastern based religions should receive a copy of BY THIS NAME. For children, a copy of THE LAMB is appropriate. We continually receive testimonies of people who came to know the Lord simply by reading a book on their own.

  It's not a bad idea to procure a copy of the various translations to have on hand if your path crosses those who do not speak English well. It is amazing how the Lord has a way of bringing such folk into your life when you have the tool available.

- **Textbook:** THE STRANGER has been found effective as a text book on the Bible for use in Bible Colleges, Christian schools, home-schools, or youth groups. It is important to use the WORKBOOK in conjunction with any school setting. I would also encourage you to use visual aids. For schools, the answers can be removed from the back of the coil-bound edition if you don't want your student "peeking." One can use the same techniques as described on page 58, under Home Bible Study.

THE STRANGER, ALL THE PROPHETS or BY THIS NAME is also being used as a textbook for missionary candidates investigating service with home or overseas ministries. These book introduces students to a system of communicating the Bible to the biblically-illiterate.

- **Correspondence Course:** As a pastor or youth worker, it is sometimes hard to know where a person stands regarding the gospel. THE STRANGER OR ALL THE PROPHETS combined with the CORRESPONDENCE COURSE allows you to operate a church or youth-based ministry. An agreed-upon schedule can be set up. (Remember: don't stretch the study over too long a period of time.) The student can progress through the material on his own time with the pastor or youth worker providing accountability. As one directing the CORRESPONDENCE COURSE, the pastor or youth worker can check the course answers and use it as a point of contact and further discussion with the student. (Remember: don't get off on side issues or jump ahead of the story.)

- **Community College Course:** Those who have gained experience in teaching the TERM curriculum in a home setting can branch out and offer an "Intro to the Bible" course at a local community college or night school. One can use the same techniques as described on page 98, under Home Bible Study. To take on this level of teaching, we would strongly suggest that you attend the TERM Seminar at least twice and master the use of the visual aids.

- **Church Sunday School:** To be honest, this is my least favorite environment for teaching TERM. The dynamics of Sunday School classes are such that the one-day-a-week class is usually limited to 45 to 50 minutes with attendance being somewhat sporadic. This violates some key principles we have discussed:

1. The entire course is spread over a long period of time, much greater than the recommended 4 to 6 weeks. Instead of having the feel of one study that is tied together, the TERM teaching becomes fragmented and each study tends to stand alone, disconnected from past lessons.

2. Due to time constraints, the material covered in each session is minimal necessitating more review which then lengthens the time to cover the total content.

3. Key building blocks of information are missed because students are not there for every class. This breaks down the continuity of the material covered, even for those who have a fairly good Bible background.

4. Because most Sunday School classes are comprised of believers, there is a tendency to want to discuss content and get off on other subjects.

For these reasons, we have seen it fail over and over again in the Sunday School environment. I have heard folk say, "Oh, we really enjoyed your book. We only got up to Chapter 11 before we took our summer break, but it was sure good!" Well, if you review the chart on page 51, you see that they missed the most critical conclusion to the entire study.

So, can TERM be used in a Sunday School setting? Yes, it can, if everyone involved understands the obstacles. The following guidelines have been built on experience. I suggest you take them seriously and not attempt to reinvent the wheel. Here are some suggestions:

1. If it is an adult class, have the known believers read this book before starting. You will need their cooperation to keep the class on course.

2. In your first session, discuss upfront the need for continuity in a Bible study of this nature. Emphasize that this is not a typical Bible course where each lesson stands on its own.

3. Obtain from your audience a commitment to stay current with the lesson by doing the questions in the **WorkBook**. They can read portions they missed or "catch up" by watching the missed material on **The Stranger** DVD. Staying current is critical for the study to make sense.

4. Ask for permission to meet a full 55 minutes or more. This may mean restructuring the class time. In one group I taught, the students came early and then skipped the Sunday school opening exercises. Snacks and coffee were available.

5. Assuming you have 55 minutes of teaching time, divide the class hour as follows:

   a) 10 minutes for review of **WorkBook** questions

   b) 40 minutes for new material

   c) 5 minutes to assign questions in **WorkBook**

6. If using **The Stranger** DVD, see pages 60-61 for schedule.

7. In teaching TERM, watch out that you stick tenaciously to the content and not be sidetracked. Believers are notorious for sidetracking the study.

If you follow this advice, you will find the study quite fruitful.

Before I leave this category of use, I want to suggest one other alternative approach. It does require a high level of commitment from the class, but it has worked quite well when the assigned time for study is limited. Here it is:

1. Each student is required to make a commitment to read an assigned portion of THE STRANGER on a weekly basis. Usually a complete chapter is chosen with the exception of Chapter 14 which is usually split into two weeks.

    NOTE: This approach to the TERM material will only work if this commitment is kept.

2. The student arrives at the class with the assigned chapter in THE STRANGER already read and the WORKBOOK answers completed.

3. The teacher, using the WORKBOOK, then carefully reviews the chapter in THE STRANGER that was read in the preceding week and answers any questions pertinent to that chapter. Once again, the teacher must tenaciously stick to the subject.

* **Church Bible Study:** In this type of study, I am assuming several factors: a number of folks will be in attendance, most will be believers, the study will be organized around a week day and held during the day or in the evening.

From my experience, these studies have a much higher success rate than the Sunday School environment.

1. The students are willing to take more than an hour for the lesson, often taking as much as two hours in any one session to complete this special type of Bible Study. As a result, less review is needed and the course in accomplished in a much shorter length of time.

2. If too many folk will be missing on the assigned Bible study day, then the class can be shifted to another day.

- **Home Bible Study:** One of the most effective ways we have found to share the gospel is to *read through* THE STRANGER or BY THIS NAME with a friend in a home study.

  1. The study is usually limited to the teacher and one or two unbelievers. If more unbelievers are interested, it is better to do a second study. In large groups it can be hard to track where unbelievers are at. Many will not share openly, and all it takes is one issue-oriented person to create problems in the minds of others.

  2. Sometimes Bible teachers "look down" upon the idea of reading together out loud. It is viewed as a children's approach to learning. But from our experience, reading out loud has been well received when handled properly. Above all else, this sort of reading does have scriptural precedents. The Bible says that Ezra stood in front of a large crowd and …

  … read from the Book of the Law of God, making it clear and giving the meaning so that the people could understand what was being read. Nehemiah 8:8

  It could be argued that Ezra needed to do that because folks could not read for themselves or scrolls were rare. But Paul also told Timothy to …

  … give attention to the public reading of Scripture, to exhortation and teaching. 1 Timothy 4:13 NASB

Why Timothy should be commanded to read the Word of God out loud is interesting. Was it for the same reasons given above?

Or was there another reason for it? Consider the following as it relates to reading THE STRANGER:

a) Presidents, kings and queens all resort to reading written speeches. Why? The reason is simple. They don't want to say the wrong thing or be misunderstood. Communications are consequential.

   The Gospel is the most important, consequential message in the world. Reading assures that you are accurate in your delivery of the content.

b) Reading assures that you cover all the material. You won't miss vital information.

c) When compared with the lecture format, reading results in significantly higher **retention**, using three senses instead of one. You are *seeing, speaking* and *hearing*, versus just *hearing*. Even the written page is a visual aid, and visual aids help us retain information. Have you ever told a person that you cannot find a verse in someone else's Bible, but you know right where it is located on the page in your Bible?

d) When compared with the lecture format, reading results in significantly higher **comprehension**.

e) Reading assures a minimum of preparation for the teacher which is a very big factor in today's "overdrive" society.

f) Reading provides the teacher with a means of communicating a significant volume of material with minimal fatigue. A teacher will likely do a better job. The Bible, from Genesis to Acts, covers a lot of information. However, when read, not only is an overview possible, it is very effective.

g) Reading assures a logical progression of thought even if you, as a teacher, are a little "scatter brained" that day.

h) Reading is non-intimidating. You can read some strong statements and as long as they are being read, the statements will be tolerated and the student will not feel threatened. However, if you are saying those same statements looking the student in the eye, you can have an argument on your hands.

i) Reading assures that the Holy Spirit does the work through His Word. A student can't say he or she was "moved" emotionally by the teacher's eloquence in delivering the message.

j) Reading minimizes personality "static." It helps take the focus off the teacher and places it on the written word, the message.

k) Reading lets the message speak for itself. In TERM teaching we emphasize this. Why? We believe the Word is sufficient to accomplish its purpose.

l) Reading teaches a person right from the beginning that the answers are found in the written Word which a person can learn for himself.

m) Reading subtly teaches that God gave us his message in writing.

n) It is a reality of life that *as you are taught, so you will teach.* Reading *out loud* models a means of communication that others can imitate even if they are not gifted teachers. This means of communication is transferable even at the "new born" level. It is not uncommon for students to go home and start reading the book with their children, their parents, or a friend.

o) Reading allows students to refer back to the content later to refresh their memory. They have the "whole sermon."

p) Conviction of sin is seen as coming from the Word, not because the teacher said something was "wrong."

q) Reading, when done in the right manner, focuses a person's attention on the Word, not on the ability of the one delivering the message.

r) Men often don't read well especially *out loud.* At times this holds them back from attempting to read Scripture or participate in discussion of spiritual things. We have found that reading THE STRANGER has resulted in a renewed confidence to read *out loud* in other Bible studies, as they gain experience reading in a TERM study.

s) Reading introduces new believers to the idea that reading the Scriptures is a vital and necessary vehicle for growth, a life habit to be developed.

t) Reading minimizes 'hidden agendas.' Students know that they have all the information in hand. They are not left wondering "What else is there?" The result? There is less suspicion. This is important in our 'hot sell' sensitive culture.

u) When in a group, reading helps the students keep their focus. Hearing various voices as each one reads and anticpating one's own turn, all help keep a person from losing his or her attention to the material.

Probably the most significant plus for reading is that you do not have to be a gifted teacher to do it. All you need is to be able to read *out loud* relatively smoothly. We would suggest that someone planning on using this method practice reading Scripture *out loud* for a minimum of five minutes daily. It doesn't take a brilliant or gifted teacher to be able to share the gospel by reading, but it's no use being a dull tool. Being a smooth reader, reading with expression, and giving words the right emphasis will help greatly.

In spite of all the positive points for reading, preaching and teaching are not inferior methods of communication. Far from it. What I am saying is that reading should not be excluded as a viable means of passing on the Word.

On the average, it takes 12 to 18 hours to read *out loud* through THE STRANGER. The time required depends on your own ability to read, that of your student, how often you get together, the use of the WORKBOOK, and how many visual aids you use.

FREQUENTLY ASKED QUESTIONS

MY STUDENT IS NOT COMFORTABLE READING OUT LOUD. WHAT SHOULD I DO?

Have a partner join you and read the Scripture verses instead of your student. If this is not possible, read both the text and the verses yourself.

HOW LONG SHOULD OUR READING SESSIONS BE?

The ability of your student or group to follow along with comprehension will vary. Most can read together for 45 minutes to an hour without difficulty. Two hours is not uncommon. Injecting short breaks (1 or 2 minutes) helps maintain alertness. If your student becomes tired, stop, and resume the study at another time.

MY STUDENT PRONOUNCES WORDS POORLY. WHAT SHOULD I DO?

Avoid making an issue of pronunciation—you risk embarrassing your student. Only offer correct pronunciation if asked to do so.

WHERE IS A GOOD LOCATION TO MEET WITH MY STUDENT?

Try to meet in a location where your student is comfortable and where distractions are minimal. A blaring television, ringing phones, loudspeakers, crying children, and disruptive animals, should be avoided. Meeting in your home allows you to control distractions. Also, your student might prefer a private location rather than a public setting since he or she may feel self-conscious about doing a Bible study at work or with family members around.

What if my student has questions?

You will want to avoid getting bogged down or sidetracked trying to answer questions, even good ones. Writing questions down will help satisfy your student that you are not evading his question. This also gives you more time to consider the answer without being put on the spot. A simple response such as, *"That's a good question. Let me write it down and we will come back to it"*, will demonstrate your sincerity. Most of your student's questions will be answered as you progress through The Stranger. Assure your student that you will come back to any unanswered questions after you have finished reading the book. Many questions become irrelevant as your student comes to understand the gospel clearly.

How often should I try to get together with my student?

Twice a week is good. Explain to your student that moving quickly through the material means less review and better comprehension.

What if my student wants to read ahead?

It certainly will not hurt your student to do this. However, encouraging your student to not read ahead will help maintain his interest in meeting together with you. At the same time, we know of students who have gone ahead and clearly understood the message on their own. If your student does read ahead, continue your study together to make sure there is accurate understanding. Remember, repetition is a proven educational concept.

CHAPTER 7

final thoughts

Let me conclude with a story from a sharp young lady who participated in one of the TERM studies I conducted. Upon completing the lessons she wrote the following:

"I grew up in a [religious] home—please notice I did not say a Christian home. To me, the whole concept of who God was, well, it wasn't a good picture. He was very foreign and distant to me. It was very difficult for me to understand that there was this God who loved me. I experienced great contrasts in growing up, none of which balanced each other out (i.e. going to church every week, attending a [religious] school, and growing up in an extremely abusive home.) In looking back though I am very thankful for all these experiences because as I entered college, the Lord began to tug on my life and caused me to ask many questions—and ultimately the most important question—what must I do to be saved? I was directed to "ask Jesus into my heart."

Let me inject additional information here. As a result of her seeking, she visited a church and went forward when the altar call was given. Though she said the "sinner's prayer," she told me that she really did not understand what it was all about. She came away from that experience feeling that she now had "permission to read the Bible" for herself. She continued to attend this church and began to help in the church ministry. I will let her continue her story.

"It was not difficult for me to live the 'good Christian life,' as I never was a real rebellious person. I have struggled, though, over the past three years in knowing if I was truly saved. No one I sought counsel with was able

to leave me with satisfaction as to what my eternal destiny was—this is
a terrifying thought in light of my position[1] *at the church."*

She told me how she went to the pastor seeking counsel on the issue of "assurance of salvation." He read her several Bible verses and they prayed. But still the doubts persisted. The session was repeated, as was the prayer. After several such meetings she was referred to an assistant pastor. Eventually she became so discouraged by this struggle for assurance, the pastoral staff recommended she see a Christian psychologist. This she did for a couple of years. She was diagnosed as having "chronic depression" and counseled and treated accordingly. When she finally attended the TERM seminar she was deep in financial debt as a result of this diagnosis. All this time she was helping out in the church and eventually ended up in a responsible position on the mission's committee.

As I taught the TERM seminar, I knew none of this lady's background. I carefully laid the foundation of the gospel through the Old Testament. She told me later that much of what I was teaching her was brand new information. She said that she did not understand where I was going with all this material, but she did understand the content being taught up to that day.

As we progressed into the New Testament, things began to fall into place for her. She now understood that she was a helpless sinner who could do nothing to please a holy God. Sin demanded death, both a physical separation from the body and an eternal separation from God. God's wrath abided on her because of her sin, and that wrath would be experienced for eternity in the lake of fire. But then God showed a kindness she did not deserve and provided a way to escape that holy anger on sin. He came to earth as the God-man Jesus and lived a perfect, spotless life. He had no sin-debt of His own to pay so He did not need to die. Out of His great love and mercy He took all her sin upon Himself and paid her death penalty for her. Jesus died in her place, as a substitute. God's justice was completely satisfied by that death, and Jesus was powerfully resurrected back to life. The question that remained for her was this, "Would she rest in, rely upon, put faith in that payment as being entirely sufficient for her? Would she trust in the One who had died and been resurrected so that she might live eternally?" She wrote,

"Only after this time of seeing clearly in God's Word who I am in relationship to Him and what He has done for me, have I come to grasp the reality of the finished work on the cross for me."

She told me later, *"When you read how Jesus cried out on the cross, 'It is finished,' I knew, oh I knew, it truly was finished for me too. Jesus paid it all."*

I asked her about her doubts. She said simply, *"They're gone. I don't think I would ever have had them if I had understood the gospel. The reason I was depressed was because seemingly no one could help me with my doubts, and I knew Christians weren't supposed to doubt. But the reason I had the doubts was because no one took the time to clearly explain the gospel."*

We should also note that it wasn't the hasty sinner's prayer at the church altar that saved her. Faith is built on facts and this lady didn't even know enough to understand what prayer she had prayed. To her it was no different than many other religious rituals she had performed at her church without understanding.

So just when was she born from above? I don't know "when," but obviously it was at the moment she trusted in what Jesus Christ had done for her on the cross. And since faith is always based on facts, and understanding the meaning of the gospel is directly connected to the power of the gospel, we would have to ask her when she understood the message. Only when she understood and then believed was the power of the gospel—the living Christ—evident in her life. Up till then she was still living in darkness.

Could that not be the reason why we have so many people who *claim to be Christians,* but show no evidence of it in their lives? They simply have never understood its message in the first place. May our hearts be so gripped with that fact, that in all we say and do, we may be found teaching a clear gospel. Let us not be discouraged but take heart in what the Apostle Paul penned 2000 years ago:

> *"When I came to you, brothers, I did not come with eloquence or superior wisdom as I proclaimed to you the testimony about God. For I resolved to know nothing while I was with you except Jesus Christ and him crucified.*
>
> *I came to you in weakness and fear, and with much trembling. My message and my preaching were not with wise and persuasive words, but with a demonstration of the Spirit's power, so that your faith might not rest on men's wisdom, but on God's power."*   1 Corinthians 2:1-5

[1] She had come to hold a significant position in a church of 3000 attendees.

appendix

HOW CAN I HELP OUT?

Our needs occur in two primary areas—prayer and facilitators.

1) PRAYER

GOODSEED is solely a gospel ministry, not only reaching those on our doorsteps but also extending outward into parts of the world that are very hostile to a Christian witness. As part of those who emphasize a clear gospel, we believe we are a target for the enemy's attacks. We value specific and timely prayer for all aspects of our ministry. If you desire to join our prayer team, and are willing to pray for us both as an organization and as individuals then we will do the following:

a) For those having access to a fax or E-mail, we will place you on a weekly update list that keeps abreast of pertinent prayer needs.

b) For those wishing to pray for individuals, we will team you with a GOODSEED staff member who you can pray for specifically.

2) FACILITATORS

a) **Waiting Rooms:** Are you a professional who has an office with a waiting room? Then why not place an edition of THE STRANGER on the coffee table in the waiting room. We will place a special stamp inside the front cover that tells how one can order a copy of the book.

Whether you have such an office or not, you can facilitate these tools being placed in waiting rooms. All you have to do is obtain the appropriate permissions. As a facilitator you will need to follow-up on the placing of books to make sure they are still in place and in good shape.

b) **Church Greeter:** Along with the pastor this job could well be the most important responsibility in the local church. A church greeter is in a position to offer newcomers copies of The Stranger to read in the privacy of their homes. It can be explained that THE STRANGER will help them gain a better understanding of what your church is all about.

c) **Retirement Centers:** Retirees are often great readers. They can also be very lonely. Your visit and the offer of a book will often be much appreciated.

d) **Libraries:** As a facilitator, you can work towards placing at least one copy of these tools in various libraries. There are schools, churches, colleges, ministries, prisons, halfway houses, rescue missions, municipalities, counties that have libraries, and are often willing to receive a copy of the various books or audio tapes. (The book should be filed under "A Bible Overview" and will often be placed in the "Religion" section.)

e) **Translations:** Translations of THE STRANGER, ALL THE PROPHETS and THE LAMB are available in other languages because churches and individuals served as facilitators. At any given time GOODSEED has more translations in the works than we have sponsors. It is exciting for a church to get behind a translation and make it their own—to hold the final product in hand and know that a clear gospel message is being presented in another language. We have had groups of churches combine their resources to make The Stranger available in a language.

As a facilitator, you can help draw together those who would be interested in such an opportunity—those who would be interested in providing the seed money for a translation. (Note: GOODSEED has structured its translations so that once the initial seed money is provided for a particular language group, the sales from the books provide for future reprints. Often the books can be sold at very minimal cost.)

f) **Organization:** GOODSEED is a ministry of the Lord. As an organization we rely on gifts from individuals and groups who share our goals. We are not sponsored financially by any denomination or other affiliation. All proceeds from the sale of books and videos are used for the on going development of the worldwide ministry of GOODSEED. No author receives any benefits from the sale of books. As a facilitator you can help sponsor this ministry as a blessing to the body of Christ as a whole.

g) **Personnel Partners:** Most of our GOODSEED personnel have served as overseas missionaries prior to joining this ministry and have family members and close friends who are ministering in remote places around the world. They know from experience the kind of tools missionaries need and have the technical skills to produce them. They have also seen what happens when missionaries do not have the tools they need.

To keep body and soul together while creating these tools, GOODSEED ministry personnel rely upon God's provision through sponsors who partner with them. While some of our personnel are based overseas, most reside in North America. Traditionally, Christian workers in the homeland are not as well supported as those who serve overseas. We need sponsors who will get behind those who have given their lives to see the gospel reach the ends of the earth. We have staff, often living on minimal support, working part-time to make ends meet. If you are a dentist, mechanic, farmer—anyone who can help facilitate the ministry of our staff by relieving living costs, this will certainly be appreciated.

NOTE: GOODSEED does not deduct administrative fees from sponsorship donations.

He told them, "The harvest is plentiful, but the workers are few. Ask the Lord of the harvest, therefore, to send out workers into his harvest field.
                                                      Luke 10:2

What I mean, brothers, is that the time is short.
                                                      1 Corinthians 7:29

goodseed® international

———————————— summary ————————————

WE BELIEVE ...

- **The Bible**

  ... that the Bible is God's personal message to mankind; that it consists of 66 books, each without error in the original writings.

- **God**

  ... that there is only one God, eternal, all-powerful and all-knowing. Though based in heaven, He exists everywhere at one time. He is perfect, equally loving and just—a holy lawgiver. Though one, He consists of three coequal, distinct persons—the Father, the Son, and the Holy Spirit.

- **Spirit Beings**

  ... that God created spirit beings (angels) that serve Him; that one, leading many others, rebelled. Though not nearly as powerful as God, Satan presently rules this world as an enemy of God; but in the future he will be cast into the Lake of Fire specially prepared for him and his followers.

- **Man**

  ... that man was created by God as a special friend; then rebelled and joined Satan's ranks resulting in all mankind being helplessly sinful. That sin incurs a debt payable only by physical and eternal death.

- **Salvation**

  ... that God came to earth as the God-man Jesus, lived a sinless life, and thus having no sin-debt of His own, lovingly paid man's sin-debt by dying in his place, after which He came back to life subsequently returning to heaven. That for all those who believe that Jesus died in their place, God counts His righteousness as their own, restores the friendship and freely gives them eternal life with Him.

- **The Believer's Life**

  …that the Holy Spirit lives inside those who trust in Jesus; that He is a daily teacher and friend, showing man how to avoid sin, encouraging and empowering man to live right.

- **The Church**

  …that there are many false religions and churches, but all those who trust in Jesus belong to a true invisible church, often visible as a local church.

- **Future Things**

  …that in the future Jesus will return to take those who love Him back to heaven, finally closing this world age by judging Satan and all who reject Him.

GOODSEED® is a not-for-profit organization that exists for the purpose of clearly communicating the contents of this book in this language and others. We invite you to contact us if you are interested in ongoing projects or translations.

GOODSEED® INTERNATIONAL
P. O. Box 3704
Olds, Alberta T4H 1P5
CANADA
Bus: 403 556 9955
Fax: 403 556 9950
info@goodseed.com

GOODSEED AUSTRALIA	1800 89 7333
	info.au@goodseed.com
GOODSEED CANADA	800 442 7333
	info.ca@goodseed.com
BONNESEMENCE CANADA	888 314 3623
Service en français	info.qc@goodseed.com
GOODSEED UK	0800 073 6340
	info.uk@goodseed.com
GOODSEED USA	888 654 7333
	info.us@goodseed.com

GOODSEED, THE EMMAUS ROAD MESSAGE, www.goodseed.com, and the Book / Leaf design mark are trademarks of GOODSEED INTERNATIONAL.

200612-057-10000